08736

THE MYSTERIOUS UNDERSEA WORLD

by

Jan Leslie Cook

BOOKS FOR WORLD EXPLORERS
NATIONAL GEOGRAPHIC SOCIETY

▲ BLUE ANGELFISH—
Average length 15 in (38.1 cm)

Contents

YOUNG SCUBA DIVERS *explore a ship that sank near the British Virgin Islands in 1867. Read more about their undersea adventure in Chapter 4.*

COVER: *A swimmer glides above a coral reef in the crater of an underwater volcano near the Hawaiian Islands. Below him, a red-spined sea urchin clings to a bony ridge of coral.*

Copyright © 1980 National Geographic Society
Library of Congress CIP data: p. 103

1
WIND, WAVES, AND TIDES

A single mighty wave carries a young surfer on a fast ride to shore. Sean Wingate, 13, of Hawaii, is using one of the most powerful forces of the sea. Waves move with so much energy that they help shape our coastlines. Pounding steadily over many years, they carve into solid rock. Waves also change beaches. They wash away sand at some places and add sand at others.

The ocean is always moving. It is easiest to see part of this movement by watching waves splash against a shore. But the ocean moves in other ways, too. On most shores, the level of the water rises and falls twice a day. As the water rises, it pushes slightly inland—if the shore is not too steep. Then the water falls again. This rising and falling movement is called the tide.

The constant motion of the sea has a great effect on the creatures that live in or near the water. To find what causes the sea's restlessness, you must look far beyond the shore.

FOAMING WAVE *curls above Sean Wingate, 13, as he rides a surfboard near his home in Sunset Beach, Hawaii.*

How the wind builds waves

When a storm far out at sea sends waves crashing against a shore, you can sense one of the natural forces that move the oceans—the wind.

The oceans of the world are huge. Seventy percent of the earth's surface is covered by water. So there are always storms or high winds somewhere at sea. The wind creates waves. Fierce storms may generate waves as tall as an 11-story building.

When storm winds drive high waves to shore, the waves can cause great damage. Such waves can rip out concrete piers and twist metal poles. When a big wave rolls into shallow water or is blocked by a wall or a rock, the wave moves upward instead of forward. That's why lighthouses on many coasts have steel screens protecting their lights. Waves have tossed rocks through lighthouse windows as high as 139 feet (42.4 m) above the level of the ocean!

Fortunately, great wave damage is rare. Waves do more good than harm. They circulate food to sea creatures, in the form of drifting plants and animals. They also distribute oxygen throughout the ocean.

DURING A STORM, *foaming breakers crash over exposed rocks near Monterey, California (left). Wind pushed these waves toward the land. Some waves travel halfway around the earth before they break on a shore.*

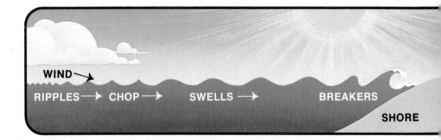

WIND → RIPPLES → CHOP → SWELLS → BREAKERS SHORE

WIND CREATES WAVES *by ruffling the ocean surface (above). As the wind continues to push the waves forward, gravity pulls them down. They form sharp peaks, or chop. If the wind dies down, the waves become rounded. Then they are called swells. Even a breeze blowing across a puddle of water will stir up waves. Tiny ripples race to the edge of the puddle and stop. In the ocean, waves keep moving until they break against a shore. Waves move at different speeds, depending on their size and how far they travel. A single wave may travel for days. When a wave reaches shallow water, its base hits the land and is slowed. But its peak continues to travel at the same speed, and soon topples over. This toppling action causes the foaming white breaker that rolls onto a beach.*

   Although a wave may travel across thousands of miles of ocean, the water itself doesn't move forward. With each passing wave, the ocean pushes up and down. Only the shape of the wave moves forward. A simple experiment will show you how a wave travels. Hold one end of a jump rope while a friend holds the other. Snap your end. A wave will travel the length of the rope.

CHASED BY THE WAVES, *two youngsters race along a Pacific Coast beach (left). The foam in the waves behind them is made up of tiny air bubbles trapped by the water. Bubbles form when wind or rain stirs up the water. When they burst, the bubbles give off a salty spray.*

7

GENTLE WAVES *ripple beyond explorers on a shore near Encinitas, California. In a few hours, water will cover the sand. Water will also cover the rocks* *where these youngsters are searching for sea life. Twice a day, at high tide, the water creeps inland. Then, at low tide, it retreats.*

How the moon tugs the tides

Have you ever noticed that the strip of land beside the sea looks narrow at some times and wide at others? The land seems to change because the level of the ocean keeps changing. Twice a day on most shorelines, the water rises very slowly. It covers part of the land. Then it slowly falls back.

This movement is called the tide. High tide covers the most land. People say, "The tide is in."

High tides usually occur about 12 hours and 25 minutes apart. Between high tides, the level of the sea slowly falls. The most land can be seen at low tide. Low tides occur about six hours after high tides. People say, "The tide is out."

Gravity is the major force that makes the water in the oceans rise and fall. When you jump up in the air, the earth's gravity pulls you down again. This gravity also holds the oceans against the earth. It keeps

WHEN THE TIDE GOES OUT *on the Pacific coast near Bolinas, California, it leaves rocks exposed.*

WHEN THE TIDE COMES IN, *few of those rocks can be seen. The ocean covers most of them.*

DUXBURY REEF *(above) shows how tides can affect a coast. Tides act differently in different places. How they act depends on the shape of the ocean floor and the slope of the land at the ocean's edge. On smooth, open beaches, the water can spread out evenly. It rises only a few feet. But in steep and narrow inlets, the water has no room to spread. So it rises sharply. The Bay of Fundy in eastern Canada has the highest tides in the world. The bay is very narrow. So the water has no place to go but up. It pushes up as much as 70 feet (21.3 m). That's about the same height as a seven-story building!*

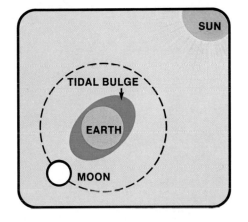

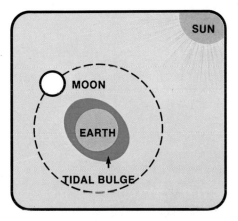

SUN POWER. *The pull of the sun and the moon affects tides. But the sun is much farther away than the moon. Its pull on the earth is not as strong. Twice a month, the sun and moon lie in a line with the earth (above). With both the sun and moon pulling together, the* tides become higher than usual. These are called spring tides. When the sun, earth, and moon form an L-shape (above), the sun and moon pull in different directions. This causes tides that rise less than usual. They are called neap tides.

the moon in orbit around the earth. The sun and the moon have gravity, too. Both pull on the earth. The moon's pull on the earth is stronger than the sun's because the moon is closer.

As the moon passes over the ocean, it pulls a bulge of water toward it. When the moon moves over land, the bulge tries to follow. Ocean water spills onto the land for a short distance. As the moon moves farther over the land, the ocean falls back.

On the side of the earth opposite the side that faces the moon, another tidal bulge moves across the ocean. This side of the earth is the farthest point from the moon. So the moon's pull is weakest here. The ocean bulges out at this weak spot, pulled by something called centrifugal force.

Centrifugal force pulls things away from a spinning center. An easy way to feel centrifugal force is to tie a large spool on the end of a long string. Then whirl the spool around in a circle. You will feel the weight of the spool pulling outward. In the same way, the ocean pulls outward from the center of the spinning earth.

EDGE OF THE SEA

2

Light from the setting sun tints a quiet beach in southern California. Shorelines weave for more than 88,000 miles along the ocean edges of the United States. Many do not look like this smooth, sandy shore near La Jolla. On some coastlines, waves splash against steep cliffs. Rocks and boulders cover others, particularly along the Pacific Ocean. Sandy beaches line much of the East Coast. A shoreline also may be formed of mud, usually left by a nearby river.

On any kind of coast, the area between the high-tide and low-tide levels is called the intertidal zone. An intertidal zone is neither ocean nor dry land, for waves wash it at least once a day. Hot sun, rain or snow, and pounding breakers make survival difficult in an intertidal zone. But many plants and animals do live here. How they adjust to this changing environment is one of the most interesting stories of the sea.

STILL WATER *reflects 7-year-*

SEASIDE SEARCH. *Young students from Del Mar, California, explore the rocky shore at nearby Encinitas. They are searching for creatures that* *remained when the tide went out. Many of the animals hide in tide pools, pockets of water trapped by the rocks. Others crawl among the seaweeds.*

Discovering the hidden life on a rocky coast

You can find a great variety of sea animals on a rocky coast. The cracks and hollows between the stones provide many cool, damp places for animals to live. Ocean creatures washed ashore by waves die quickly unless they find protection from the hot sun and pounding waves.

Rocks also provide surfaces for gripping. Animals and plants anchored on rocks are not pulled out of

EXAMINING A SNAIL. *Deanna Spooner, left, and Dana Young, both 10, inspect a smooth brown turban snail. They found the snail clinging to a piece of seaweed. Like many tide-pool creatures, snails carry protection with them. Hard shells help shield the animals from the drying sun and pounding waves. The shells also prevent some enemies from eating the snails.*

STUDYING A STAR. *Darci Moore, below left, and Julie Dodd, two 12-year-olds, let wriggly brittle stars crawl over their hands. The girls must be gentle. The arms of a brittle star break easily. But in a few months, new arms grow in their place.*

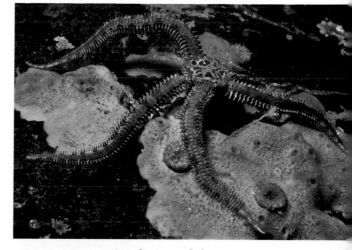

BRITTLE STAR. *A relative of the starfish, the brittle star (above) lives under rocks in tide pools. Its mouth is on the underside of its body. It finds its food by feeling for it.*

place by the waves. Many shell-covered creatures, such as limpets and chitons, have a fleshy organ called a foot. The foot sticks to a rock, like a suction cup. An oyster makes a cement-like material in its body. With this homemade glue, the oyster attaches itself firmly to a rock or a larger shell. The mussel, a relative of the oyster, spins strong, silky threads that anchor the animal to rocks.

Often, seawater collects in holes in and between the rocks to form tide pools. Waves carry young fish and invertebrates into the tide pools. Invertebrates are animals without backbones, such as the starfish.

Life can be harsh in a tide pool. The summer sun may make the water very hot. Ice may form during the winter. Creatures that can't adjust to changing conditions may die.

Plants called algae grow on the rocky shore. Seaweeds are large algae. They have root-like growths called holdfasts. The holdfasts anchor the plants to rocks. Seaweeds provide both food and shelter for many different kinds of intertidal animals. Small creatures often creep under seaweeds for protection. Soft green or red fuzz on rocks is also a kind of algae. Some sea animals graze on this fuzz.

13

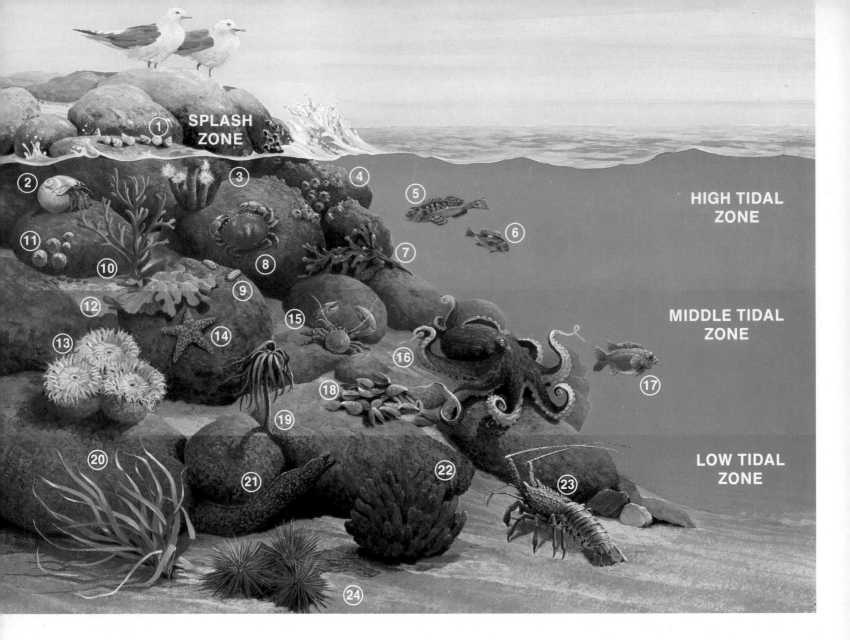

The painting above shows 24 sea animals and plants that might live in an intertidal zone. You can identify them by using the numbered list of names below.

Layers of life at a seashore

In a way, the seashore is like a tall building. But instead of floors, the shore has tidal zones. What makes one zone different from another is how long water covers it as the tides rise and fall.

Ocean invertebrates and fish need contact with water. Water contains their food and the oxygen they breathe. But some of these creatures can live for a long time out of water. Most intertidal animals stay in the zone that supplies the amount of water and food they need. Many move from zone to zone.

You can see the tidal zones most clearly on a rocky shore where the tide rises more than six feet. Water covers the low tidal zone almost all the time. It covers the middle tidal zone about half the time, and the high tidal zone only a short time. The splash zone receives only ocean spray.

(1) periwinkles
(2) hermit crab
(3) feather duster worms
(4) barnacles
(5) tide pool sculpin
(6) opaleye
(7) common rockweed
(8) rock crab
(9) chitons
(10) codium sponge seaweed
(11) limpets
(12) sea lettuce
(13) sea anemones
(14) starfish
(15) porcelain crab
(16) octopus
(17) garibaldi fish
(18) mussels
(19) sea palm
(20) eelgrass
(21) moray eel
(22) redbeard sponge
(23) spiny lobster
(24) red sea urchins

14

▲ GHOST CRAB — Average width 3 in (7.6 cm)

▲ HERMIT CRAB — Average length 3 in (7.6 cm)

An album of

SEASHORE CREATURES

Like a busy city, the seashore stirs with life. Creatures search for food or hide from enemies. Many crabs adjust well to life on shore. They move fast enough to escape enemies. Some eat almost anything. The crab above burrows in the sand during the heat of the day. At night, it hunts for food. It is called a ghost crab because its shell blends with the sand. The hermit crab has no shell. To protect its soft body, it moves into the shell of another animal. When it finds an empty shell that fits, the crab backs in. As the hermit outgrows each shell, it finds a larger one.

Some seashore animals move around to hunt for food. Others wait for food to come to them. The sea anemone has arms called tentacles around its mouth. The tentacles contain stinging cells that paralyze small animals that brush against them. Then the tentacles slowly draw the animals into the anemone's mouth. The island kelpfish often lives in shallow water. It usually stays in one area. If smaller fish enter its territory, the kelpfish chases them away. Other creatures, such as the chiton, eat plants. Eight hard plates form the chiton's flexible shell. Its body fits snugly against a rock. The chiton and the top snail scrape algae from rocks. Purple urchins also eat algae. Their stiff spines can injure a wader.

▲ ISLAND KELPFISH—Average length 4 in (10.2 cm)

▲ SEA ANEMONE—Average diameter 4 in (10.2 cm)

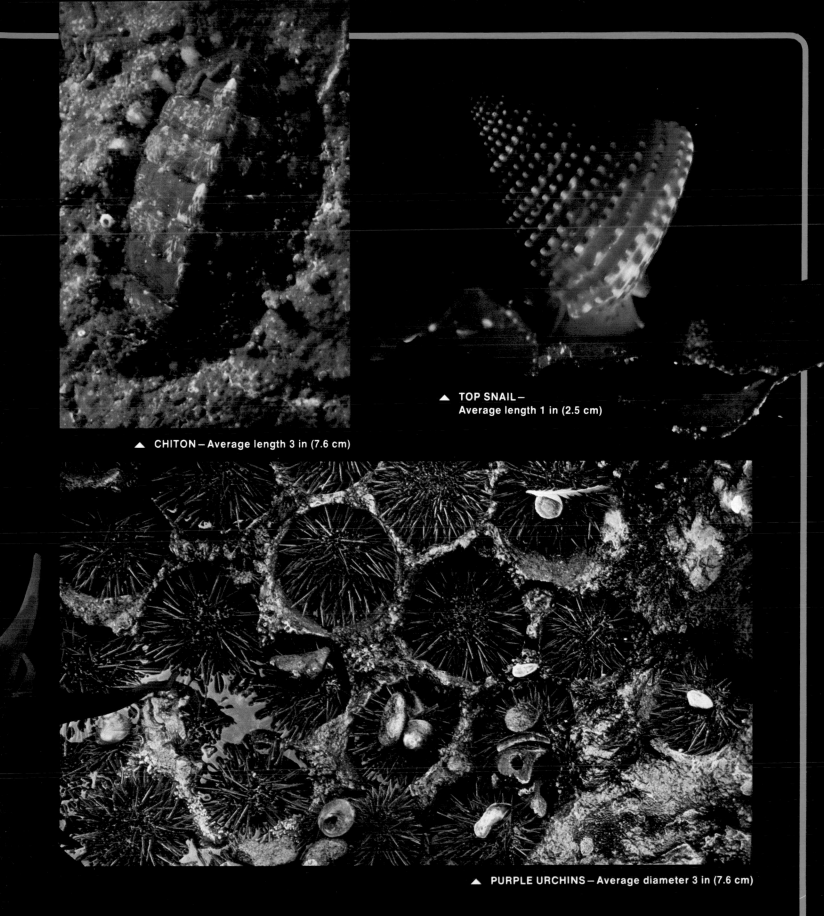

▲ CHITON — Average length 3 in (7.6 cm)

▲ TOP SNAIL —
Average length 1 in (2.5 cm)

▲ PURPLE URCHINS — Average diameter 3 in (7.6 cm)

17

Watery forests of giant kelp

On some Pacific shores, you might see long ribbons of seaweed lying on the beach. Often it is giant kelp that the waves have washed ashore. Giant kelp grows offshore. But it can be part of the intertidal-zone community, too. Giant kelp produces gas-filled bladders (right). The bladders float the top of the plant to the surface where it gets the light it needs to grow. Kelp provides food and shelter for many kinds of creatures, such as snails and fish.

Trees that build beaches

A red mangrove tree sends its arching roots into a muddy shore near Miami, Florida (below). Mangroves help keep such shores from washing away. The trees build land, too. They trap mud, sand, and shells among their roots (far right). Mangroves provide homes for many animals, including crabs, oysters, and shrimps. A mangrove seed sprouts before it drops from the tree. The young plant may float for a long time before taking root in shallow water (right). Then it grows quickly, as much as two feet in a year.

Uncovering the life on a sandy beach

Walking along a sandy beach, you might think that few animals could live there. All you see is a gentle slope of sand that gradually disappears beneath the waves. Perhaps dunes, dry hills of sand covered with waving grass, line the inland side of the beach. There are very few rocks to trap seaweeds or to protect small animals from the sun and the waves.

Actually, many creatures live on a sandy beach. Most stay underground where it is damp and cool. Millions of tiny animals live in the water that collects between the grains of sand. Larger creatures also burrow into the sand. You may recognize some familiar sandy-beach residents in the pictures below.

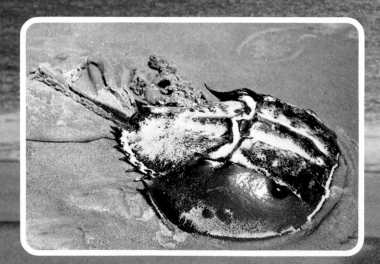

HORSESHOE CRAB. *Empty horseshoe-crab shells often litter sandy beaches. This animal isn't really a crab. Its only relative is the spider. The horseshoe crab burrows into the sand hunting for food, such as worms. It may be as long as 20 inches (50.8 cm) from head to tail.*

COQUINAS. *Clams called coquinas are usually less than an inch long. Like all clams, coquinas are bivalves. Two matching shells are joined by a hinge. With a muscular foot, a coquina burrows into the sand. It pushes a tube toward the surface that collects food and water.*

BEACH VISITORS. *Two sea lions wade at a California beach. These mammals are common along the western shores of the United States.*

SAND CRAB. *The sand crab lives at the edge of the ocean. It grows little more than an inch long. A sand crab catches food with its tentacles. The female sand crab produces thousands of bright-orange eggs.*

SAND DOLLAR. *This relative of the sea urchin is only a skeleton. A living sand dollar is covered with short, flexible spines. The spines help it move around on the surface and dig into the sand.*

Stormy weather brings an unusual visitor

Roz and Daniel Emmett were watching a storm from their California beach house. Suddenly they saw something waddle ashore. It was a young sea lion! It climbed up on their deck and stayed for a visit. Roz, 6, and Daniel, 7, named the visitor Herby.

Herby had an infection when he came ashore. The Emmetts took him to the nearby Santa Barbara Zoo where he could be treated. Now well, Herby still lives there. And now the Emmetts visit him!

ANYBODY HOME? *Herby eyes the deck of the Emmett house in California (left). "We saw him climb up on the deck," said Roz Emmett. "We were so surprised! He stayed for ten days."*

DOWN THE HATCH. *"Herby gobbled up six fish a day," Roz said. "He ate them whole. We took turns feeding him. Neighbors gave us the fish."*

ROZ DELIVERS LUNCH *to Herby (left). "We saw seals swim by, but none ever came near our house before," she said. "No one believed me when I told my class about Herby. I had to show pictures of him."*

KEEPING COOL, *Herby naps under the deck. "We decided that Herby came ashore because he wasn't strong enough to survive a storm," said Daniel Emmett. "It was fun to have him at our house. I'm glad he's nearby at the zoo so we can see him often."*

Enjoying sea life without destroying it

Without wildlife, the shore would be a less interesting place. Yet some creatures are disappearing. They are victims of pollution and uncontrolled fishing and collecting. Today, laws protect some threatened animals. One law forbids the capture of seals and whales, including dolphins, without permission.

A California law protects fish called grunion. These fish come ashore at night to lay their eggs. Many people eat grunion. The law says the fish may be caught only by hand. People cannot catch them in April or May, when most egg-laying occurs. That way, enough grunion survive to return the next year.

FISHING BY HAND, *Californians catch grunion (above, right). The fish come ashore at night to lay eggs in the sand (right). A female can lay as many as 3,000 eggs in less than a minute!*

24

OFFERING FOOD, *bathers on the western coast of Australia make friends with gentle dolphins (left). These rubbery-skinned animals seem to enjoy human company. They often race beside boats and* sometimes play hide-and-seek with divers. Dolphins can't breathe underwater. They must come to the surface regularly for air. They breathe through the blowholes on their heads.

SHELL COLLECTOR. *Nine-year-old Steve Sarkin studies a seashell (right). Steve lives in Hollywood, Florida. He began collecting shells along the beach when he was 5. Now he has almost 500 different kinds. Each time Steve finds a new shell, he identifies it by finding its picture in one of his books about shells. The books also tell him about the animals that once lived in the shells. For example, the flame scallop (above, right) uses its brightly colored tentacles to sense danger. If an enemy such as a starfish threatens, the scallop forces a powerful stream of water from between its shells and jets away.*

25

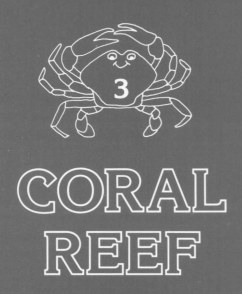

3 CORAL REEF

Chris Dobbins and Kevin O'Conner can glide through the water almost as easily as a pair of fish. They wear gear that helps them do it: swim fins and breathing tubes called snorkels.

Chris, 13, far right, and Kevin, 12, are snorkeling at John Pennekamp Coral Reef State Park. Pennekamp is the world's first all-underwater park. It lies three miles off Key Largo, Florida, where Chris and Kevin live.

Pennekamp contains part of the only living coral reef in the United States. A coral reef is an underwater ridge built by tiny animals called coral polyps. The polyps form the ridge with a hard substance produced by their bodies. The polyps live on the surface of the reef.

Coral reefs occur in shallow water in some warm areas of the ocean. They attract a large variety of sea life. When Chris and Kevin snorkel at Pennekamp park, they visit a colorful and ever-changing undersea world.

UNDERSEA EXPLORERS. *Kevin O'Conner and Chris Dobbins glide through sunlit water near Key Largo, Florida.*

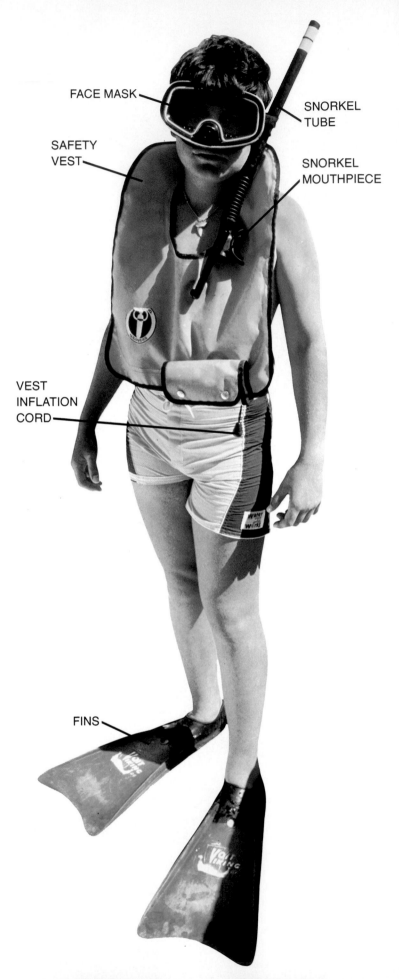

FACE MASK

SNORKEL TUBE

SAFETY VEST

SNORKEL MOUTHPIECE

VEST INFLATION CORD

FINS

MASK TIPS. *Larry Gavagni, a park ranger at John Pennekamp Coral Reef State Park, explains to Chris and Kevin how a face mask should fit.*

Taking a first step into the sea

Before exploring Pennekamp reef, Chris and Kevin learned to snorkel with experts. Both youngsters swim well and wear the proper gear. If you are a good swimmer, you can try snorkeling, too. The YMCA, the YWCA, and shops that sell diving gear sometimes offer classes.

To snorkel, you'll need the equipment that Kevin wears (right). An important item is a rubber mask with a glass window. Before buying a mask, put it on and inhale through your nose. If air leaks in, the mask doesn't fit. A rubber snorkel should feel comfortable in your mouth. You'll also need a flotation vest for safety. You inflate the vest by blowing into a tube or by pulling a cord attached to a pocket. The vest will keep you afloat. Swim fins make swimming much easier. The fins also protect the soles of your feet from cuts and stings. Now you're ready to follow Chris and Kevin as they jump in and take a close look at a coral reef.

SNORKEL FACTS. *A snorkel is a J-shaped rubber tube with a mouthpiece attached to the curved end. It lets a swimmer breathe while looking down into the water. You can see one way to use it at right. Gripping the mouthpiece between your teeth, put your head underwater. Be careful to keep the straight end of the snorkel above the* *surface. By breathing through the snorkel, you can watch the ocean beneath you without raising your head. If you want to dive below the surface, take a deep breath and hold it during the dive. As soon as you come back up to the surface, blow a big puff of air through the snorkel. That should clear the water from the tube.*

LESSONS OVER, *Kevin, Gavagni, and Chris prepare to make an underwater tour of Pennekamp coral reef (below). Rangers like Gavagni patrol the 21 miles of* reef *that make up the park. State law forbids taking or harming anything in the park. The rangers see that visitors observe the law.*

Drifting above Pennekamp reef, Chris, Kevin, and Larry Gavagni look down on a brightly colored jumble of corals, fish, and other creatures.

Kevin has snorkeled for eight years. He helps his dad, who runs a boat that takes visitors diving and snorkeling. Chris works at a marina. She pumps gas

for motor boats. Both youngsters snorkel whenever they have the chance.

"When I show visitors the reef for the first time, they are usually surprised at how colorful it is," Kevin says. "I guide them around and point out things that could sting or bite them. I often take

CORAL COMMUNITY. *Just a few feet below the surface, Gavagni points out a group of lacy sea fans (left). Sea fans are corals, but they don't build reefs. They have leathery bodies that wave gently with the movement of the water, like trees swaying in a breeze. Because sea fans bend, they rarely break when a storm stirs up the water. In some places they form a protective shield over the reef.*

DIVING DEEPER. *Chris, Kevin, and Gavagni glide between living boulders of star coral (below). The snorkelers kick gently to avoid frightening the fish swimming nearby. Before this part of the reef became a protected state park, visitors sometimes chipped off pieces of coral to take home. This often killed the remaining coral. "People can damage coral just by touching it," says Gavagni. "Coral is delicate. A cut can harm a coral formation just as it can injure human skin."*

people to a place called Hole in the Wall. There they can actually swim through a gap in the coral."

Kevin has an aquarium and a shell collection at home. When his class at school studied undersea life, Kevin found that he already knew most of the facts in his textbook.

GORGONIAN CORAL — Average length 2-3 ft (61-91 cm)

An album of
CREATURES OF A CORAL REEF

Lacy branches of coral wave in the moving ocean. This coral forms part of a complex community of plants and animals. Flexible, tree-shaped corals grow in seas all over the world.

This one lies near a rock-hard coral reef off the coast of Australia. Called the Great Barrier Reef, it stretches for 1,250 miles (2,011 km). It is the largest coral reef in the world. The corals that built it are called hard, or stony, corals. Reef-building corals live only in warm, clear, shallow water. So you usually find reefs near a shore and parallel to it. Some coral reefs rise above the surface of the water and form islands.

Reefs shelter thousands of living creatures. Clams and sponges attach themselves to the stony corals. Tiny plants called algae grow in cracks and small openings. Worms, crabs, and many kinds of colorful fish move in and out of holes in the uneven surface. Octopuses and moray eels find hiding places in larger caves.

Although reef coral is very hard, coral reefs are easily damaged. Pounding waves and some starfish are natural causes of destruction. But people are especially dangerous. Fishing and pollution can upset the fragile reef system.

Coral communities:
How they live and grow

Corals grow in hundreds of different shapes, sizes, and colors. Each of the corals on these two pages is really a clump, or colony, of tiny animals called polyps. Most of the polyps are so small they measure less than an inch across. But these polyps divide and form other polyps. Together, they can build coral colonies that extend for many hundreds of feet.

Each polyp has a soft body with tentacles at the top. A hard, cup-shaped skeleton protects it. At night, the polyp stretches out its tentacles to trap food. Some corals sting and eat very small fish. Most live on plankton, tiny drifting plants and animals. By day, the polyp closes up. It pulls its tentacles into its skeleton.

Polyps anchor themselves to the ocean floor or to some other firm surface. Young polyps attach themselves to older ones. As polyps of hard coral die, new polyps grow on their remains. The remains slowly pile up into a huge mass that may form the base of a reef.

◀ *DENDRONEPHTHYA* SOFT CORAL —
Average height 8-12 in
(20.3-30.5 cm)

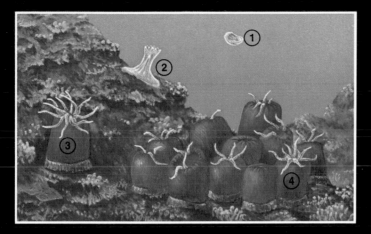

BUILDING A CORAL REEF. *A reef begins when the egg of a hard coral hatches into a larva. This larva drifts through the water (1) until it settles onto a hard surface. There it produces a limy, cup-shaped skeleton (2). The cup protects the larva and anchors it in place. When the larva is three weeks old, it becomes a polyp (3). Tentacles sprout from the top. Soon the polyp splits into two polyps. Then each polyp splits again. As the polyps continue to multiply, the reef slowly grows (4). Sometimes clumps of coral break off and form new colonies.*

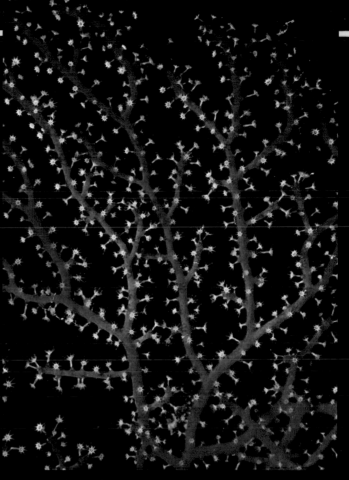

▲ GORGONIAN CORAL — Average length 2-3 ft (61-91 cm)

◄ *LEPTASTREA PURPUREA* CORAL —
Average diameter of each polyp 1/2-1 in (1.3-2.5 cm)

▲ ELKHORN CORAL —
Average width 6-10 ft (1.8-3.1 m)

35

Close-knit crowds and lone hunters

Coral reefs provide a fertile feeding ground for all kinds of ocean life. Below, a school of fish eats plankton around a reef in the Caribbean.

These purple-blue creole wrasses are among nearly 2,000 kinds of fish that swim together in large groups, or schools. The brightly colored golden-headed wrasse is also a schooling fish.

Schooling fish usually swim together in groups of hundreds or even thousands. Each group has a definite organization. Each fish stays a certain distance from the others. If a fish leaves the school to get food, the others will follow. Like rows of marching soldiers, the entire school may suddenly shift direction.

Fish form schools for several reasons. It is easier to find a mate in a large group. It is also

▲ CREOLE WRASSE—
Average length 12 in (30 cm)

▲ GOLDEN-HEADED WRASSE—Average length 7 in (17.5 cm)

safer to live in a school. The motion of a large number of tiny fish swimming together may confuse an enemy. Even if the enemy attacks, each fish has a better chance to get away.

Other reef-dwellers live by themselves. The moray eel is a fish with a long, muscular body. This ferocious-looking creature hides in a hole in a coral reef during the day. It darts out at night to snatch food in its sharp teeth. The moray feeds on crabs and small octopuses and squid.

The octopus, too, creeps out of its reef home after dark to look for food. Using eight long arms, it pulls itself across the ocean floor. Suction cups on the undersides of the arms help pry open shellfish. If an enemy attacks, the octopus shoots inky liquid from its body. This may confuse an enemy with poor eyesight, such as the moray eel. The ink forms a shape that resembles an octopus. While its enemy attacks the ink blob, the octopus escapes.

SHARP TEETH *and open jaws give the moray eel (left) a fierce appearance. Actually, this eel is not attacking anything. It must open and close its mouth to breathe. Moray eels are large. Most grow four to five feet (1.2-1.5 m) long. Some may even reach ten feet (3 m). Shy creatures, they do not attack people unless they are disturbed.*

IN HIDING. *The shy octopus (below) changes its color to match its surroundings. The creature also turns pale when frightened. Sometimes it escapes danger by squeezing its boneless body through a small opening. It can also shoot water from its body and rocket backward. A few octopuses measure 16 feet (4.8 m) from their heads to the tips of their arms. Many measure 2 to 3 feet (60-90 cm). Others are smaller.*

Brightly colored swimmers

Sparkling like polished blue gemstones, damselfish drift above pink coral. Many fish that live near coral reefs have bright colors. The colors may help the fish survive by hiding them from enemies or from creatures they hunt as food.

No two kinds of fish look exactly alike. Each has special patterns of colors, spots, or stripes. Some scientists think the different patterns help fish recognize others of their kind among the thousands of fish near a coral reef.

▲ HARLEQUIN WRASSE—Average length 10 in (25 cm)

▲ SPECKLED BOX FISH—Average length 6 in (15 cm)

▼ DAMSELFISH—Average length 4 in (10 cm)

▲ TRUMPETFISH—Average length 36 in (90 cm)

▲ FAIRY BASSLET—Average length 3 in (7.6 cm)

▲ ANGLERFISH—Average length 4 in (10 cm)

▲ BLUE-STRIPED ANGELFISH—Average length 12 in (30 cm)

Soft-bodied nibblers and trappers of food

Many creatures living on a reef have unusual shapes. The sponge below resembles a flower vase. The anemone beside it looks like a colorful flower. Actually, both are animals.

Sponges often anchor themselves to coral. Sponges provide homes for other creatures of the reef. Shrimps and small fish may live in openings in the sponges' bodies.

The sponge is sometimes called the filter of the sea because of the way it gets its food. Each day, the sponge pumps hundreds of gallons of water through tiny holes in its body. As it does, it filters plankton from the water.

STRAWBERRY SPONGE ▲
Average height 12 in (30 cm)

Bright sea slugs like those below have feathery tentacles called cerata. The cerata are probably used for finding food and for breathing. Some sea slugs, like the one at left, breathe through branching gills. The gills take oxygen from the water. Marine worms (bottom) stretch out tree-like arms to trap plankton. When danger threatens, the worms quickly pull in their arms.

▲ DORID NUDIBRANCH—Average length 1.5 in (3.8 cm)

▲ AEOLID NUDIBRANCHS—Average length 1.5 in (3.8 cm)

▲ POLYCHAETE WORMS—Average width 1/2 in (1.3 cm)

◀ ANEMONE—Average diameter 3-4 in (7.6-10.2 cm)

41

Creatures with arms, spines, and claws

Living starfish look different from the stiff, pale skeletons that wash up on shore. Alive, these creatures have flexible, colorful bodies.

Most starfish have five arms. But some have as many as 45. If an arm breaks off, another grows in its place. Rows of tubes line the bottom of each arm. The tips of the tubes act as suction disks. The starfish uses suction to pull open the shells of clams or oysters. It can hold on for hours. When it has opened the shells a tiny bit, the starfish pushes its stomach between the shells and eats the animal inside.

The sea urchin, a relative of the starfish, has stiff spines. The spines protect the urchin from hungry fish as it nibbles on algae.

▼ RED SEA STARFISH — Average diameter 10 in (25 cm)

▼ SLATE-PENCIL SEA URCHIN — Average diameter 6 in (15 cm)

▼ COBALT BLUE STARFISH — Average diameter 5-6 in (13-15 cm)

The crab has a tough shell and two strong claws for protection. If the crab loses a claw in a fight, it grows a new one. A crab's hard shell does not grow. As the crab becomes larger, it sheds its covering again and again. Just before the old shell comes off, a new, soft one forms beneath it. The shedding process is called molting. Until the new shell hardens, which takes from three hours to three days, the crab has no armor to protect it. It must hide from enemies.

Many different kinds of crabs live in the ocean. Some are less than a quarter of an inch long. But the giant spider crab may reach ten feet (3 m) from claw tip to claw tip. Besides shells and claws, some crabs have other ways of protecting themselves. The boxer crab scares off enemies by carrying a stinging sea anemone in each claw. Some hermit crabs place anemones on top of their shells as live-on bodyguards. Anemones help keep unwanted visitors away. The decorator crab plants a seaweed garden on top of its shell. The seaweed makes the crab difficult to spot as it crawls among the plants on the ocean floor.

▲ RED CRAB — Average width 6 in (15 cm)

Portrait gallery of odd-shaped faces

This picture gallery of undersea faces might make some people laugh. The faces look funny, and so do some of the bodies attached to them. But odd features, colors, and shapes usually serve an important purpose. They may help an animal fit into its surroundings. A sharp beak makes it easy to nibble algae. Large eyes can see well in dim light. A skinny body can fit into small hiding places.

The decorated prickleback often backs into holes in the reef. When only its head shows, the threads above its eyes may look like plants growing on the reef. The blue ribbon eel can curl its thin body around rocks and coral. The smooth trunkfish blows water into the sand through spout-like lips. The blast uncovers burrowing creatures that the trunkfish eats. Both the honeycomb cowfish and the unicorn tang have horns on their heads. The horns help protect the cowfish's eyes as it attacks crabs. The unicorn tang's horn may help it attract a mate.

▲ HONEYCOMB COWFISH—
Average length 13 in (33 cm)

▲ BLUE RIBBON EEL—Average length 36 in (90 cm)

UNICORN TANG—
Average length 20 in (50 cm) ▼

▲ DECORATED PRICKLEBACK—
Average length 16 in (40 cm)

SMOOTH TRUNKFISH—
Average length 12 in (30 cm) ▶

45

UNDERSEA ADVENTURE

After exploring the world just below the surface, many snorkelers want to see more. They want to dive deeper and stay underwater longer. They may want to explore a shipwreck on the seafloor. With equipment called scuba, they can!

Scuba stands for self-contained underwater breathing apparatus. Scuba consists of air tanks and other equipment that divers wear. Underwater, the divers breathe air from the tanks. Because they don't have to come up for air, they can swim freely underwater for an hour or more.

Beginning scuba divers have a lot to learn. They have to get used to moving underwater, and they must be familiar with their gear. They also must learn important safety rules.

For these reasons, people who want to scuba dive should take lessons first. Students practice diving many times in shallow water before they try scuba diving in the ocean.

WEARING SCUBA GEAR, *a diver enters a world of fish while exploring a coral reef in the Red Sea.*

FIRST LESSON. *Instructor George Marler explains how to use a face mask (above). His students are, from the left, Hector Penn, 15, Paul Glowasky, 11, and Alice and Cathy MacKenzie, 13 and 15. All live in the British Virgin Islands.*

GEARING UP. *Marler shows his students a regulator (above). The regulator controls the amount and the pressure of air that flows from the tank. A scuba diver may also carry a watch, a knife, a compass, and a depth gauge.*

Preparing to enter a watery world

"If you think you've seen everything, go scuba diving," says 15-year-old Hector Penn, of Tortola, in the British Virgin Islands. "The ocean is a whole different world."

Scuba lessons can be your ticket to that world. Scuba diving is a little like floating in space. You must carry your atmosphere with you. And you must know how to avoid unusual dangers that exist only in this strange environment.

Although you don't feel it, air has weight. At sea level, it pushes against every square inch of your body with a pressure of 14.7 pounds (1 kg per sq cm). You don't feel this pressure because air inside your body pushes out with equal pressure. Water at sea level weighs almost 800 times as much as air. As you dive deeper, the water becomes even heavier.

A scuba tank is filled with compressed air, air that is squeezed under pressure into a small space. As you dive, air is released from the tank into a regulator in the breathing tube. The regulator keeps the air at the same pressure as that of the surrounding water. By breathing this air, your lungs push out with the same force as water exerts as it presses in. This keeps your lungs from being crushed.

Every scuba diver must know how to decompress before surfacing. Decompressing means letting your body adjust to decreasing water pressure. Most divers do it by returning to the surface slowly. Water pressure forces the body to hold in a gas called nitrogen. If you surface slowly, the nitrogen leaves your body naturally. You exhale it through your lungs. But if you return to the surface too quickly, the nitrogen forms bubbles in your body. This condition is painful, and can be fatal. Divers call it the bends.

On these pages, a diving instructor shows some beginners how to have a safe scuba adventure.

BUDDY BREATHING. *Hector practices sharing his air supply with his teacher (left). If Hector runs out of air or his gear fails during a dive, he can buddy breathe with another diver until they safely reach the surface. In an emergency, buddy breathing can save a diver's life.*

WITH A HAND SIGNAL, *Marler and his pupils show that they are ready to begin their ocean dive. The flag at the left is* *flown over an area where divers are underwater. It warns people on boats that there are divers below: Approach with caution!*

First steps into the sea

Divers searched for centuries for a way to breathe underwater. Early divers breathed through hollow plant stems that extended to the surface. Ancient Greeks invented the diving bell. The bell was like an upside-down bucket forced underwater. Divers breathed air trapped inside. Later, diving helmets were invented. Air reached the divers through hoses from the surface. In 1865, some divers also wore air cans (right). If a hose broke, the can held enough air to get the diver to the surface.

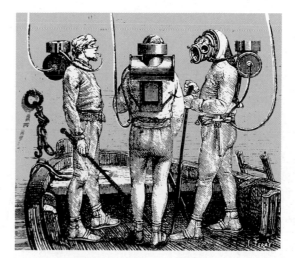

49

GROUND RULES. *Before touring R.M.S. Rhone National Park, divers read the park rules on an underwater sign. The sign warns visitors not to harm or remove any of the animals or plants that live in the park. R.M.S. stands for Royal Mail Steamer, a British mail carrier.*

SUNKEN SHIP. *At the stern, or rear section, of the* Rhone *(left), Paul and Alice inspect the room that held the ship's engine gears. The* Rhone *sank near the British Virgin Islands in 1867. It broke into five pieces. This wreck is a popular spot for divers. It is well preserved and close to shore. Parts lie within 15 feet (4.5 m) of the surface.*

CLOUDS OF BUBBLES *follow Marler and the students as they glide over a shallow coral reef 20 feet (6 m) below the surface. The undersea world appears blue because water blocks out some kinds of light rays more quickly than others. Red rays begin to vanish close to the surface. Orange and yellow rays fade soon after. Blue and green rays reach to 130 feet* (39.6 m). *Beyond that depth, the sea begins to darken. At about 3,000 feet (900 m), it is totally black. Water changes other things, too. It makes objects look larger and closer than they really are. A nearby fish that looks a foot (30 cm) long actually may be several inches shorter. The fish also may be farther away than it seems.*

51

UNDERWATER LAMPS *light up the bow, or front end, of the Rhone. The ship lies on its side. Sponges, corals, and sea fans cover the wreck. "The Rhone attracts a lot of fish," says Paul. "I've seen tangs and triggerfish there, and sometimes eels."*

SEA LIFE quickly takes over a shipwreck like the Rhone *(right). Corals and sponges attach themselves to exposed surfaces. Fish find hiding places in and around the shadowy skeleton—and attract other creatures that feed on them.*

BRITISH STEAMER. *The* Rhone *(above) was only two years old when it sank during a hurricane. A sturdy ship, the* Rhone *was plated with steel and powered by steam. It traveled between South America and England. Usually it stopped for fuel and cargo in the British Virgin Islands. The* Rhone *was anchored there on October 29, 1867, when a hurricane struck. The winds tore the ship loose from its 3,000-pound (1,360 kg) anchor and swept it out to sea. There it struck rocks and sank. In all, 123 passengers and crewmen were lost. To protect the remains of the* Rhone, *the government has created a national park at the wreck site.*

INSIDE THE WRECK, *the divers explore the* Rhone's *cargo room (right). Once this room held gold and other goods being shipped to England. Divers removed most of the cargo soon after the ship sank. But a few pieces of gold may remain, buried in the wreckage.*

An album of
OFFSHORE DWELLERS

Sandy, a spotted dolphin, greets divers near San Salvador, in the Bahama Islands. A wild dolphin, Sandy appeared one day and began to play with divers. He stayed around for a year. Then he left, probably to join other dolphins.

People have a special interest in these intelligent animals. Dolphins have an ability that would help human divers. Dolphins find their way while underwater by making squeals and listening for echoes. The echoes tell the dolphins what is nearby. This sound system works somewhat like radar. It helps the dolphins stay alive. Many other sea creatures have unusual ways of protecting themselves. You will see some of these defenses on the next pages.

Working together for food, health, or safety

In the sea, as on land, animals must find enough food to stay alive. They also must protect themselves. Many sea animals depend on other creatures for food or for protection.

The clown fish (above) swims among the stinging tentacles of a sea anemone. Yet the fish is unharmed. A natural coating on its body

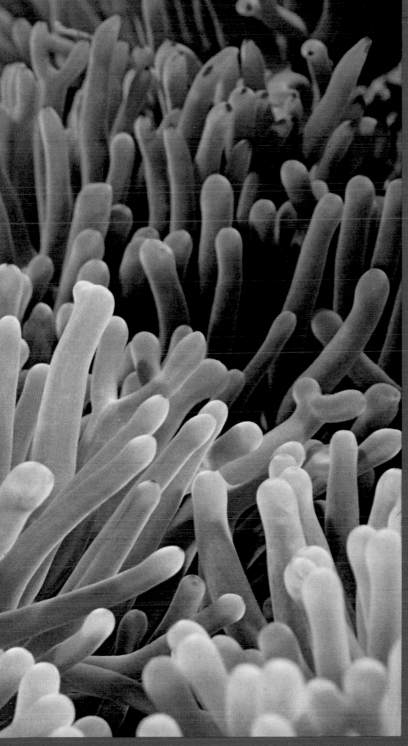

▲ CLOWN FISH — Average length 3.8 in (9.7 cm)

▲ GOBY — Average length 2 in (5.1 cm)

protects it. Scientists think the clown lures food to the anemone and then eats the leftovers.

Several kinds of small fish operate cleaning services for larger fish. The little cleaners even serve customers that often eat small fish. A goby removes food from the teeth of a grouper (top right). As a result, the goby has a meal,

and the large fish receives free dental care.

One goby (above) serves as a "seeing eye" fish for a blind shrimp. The shrimp digs an underground den and fishes for food at the entrance. The goby watches outside for enemies. When danger threatens, the goby dives into the den. The shrimp feels the motion and follows.

Dressing up for dinner – or puffing up to avoid it

Disguised as a salad, a decorator crab stays on the lookout for dinner (right). This crab uses its claws to cut off pieces of plant-like animals called hydrozoans. Then the crab attaches the feathery pieces to hooks on its shell. The crab also may hang seaweeds on its shell.

The porcupine fish (below, right) was named for the quill-covered land animal. Usually, the sharp spines of this fish lie flat. But when the porcupine is frightened, it gulps water. Then its body puffs up to three times its normal size. This pushes out the spines, which may frighten away a hungry enemy. If the enemy attacks anyway, it may spit out the fish, as the grouper below seems ready to do.

▲ DECORATOR CRAB — Average length 12 in (30.4 cm)

▲ BLACK GROUPER —
Average length 3 ft (91.4 cm)

PORCUPINE FISH — Length from 1 in to 3 ft (2.5-90 cm) ▶

58

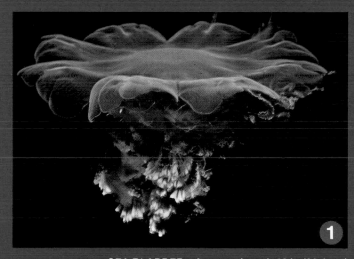

▲ SEA BLADDER — Average length 12 in (30.4 cm)

▲ FIRE CORAL — Maximum width of blade 6 in (15.4 cm)

▲ GEOGRAPHY CONE — Average length 3.5 in (8.9 cm)
▼ STONEFISH — Average length 9 in (22.9 cm)

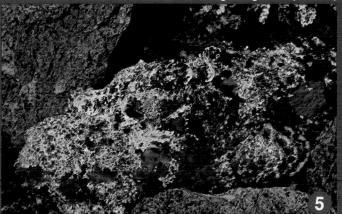

Divers beware!
Creatures to avoid

1 *Fiery pain tells many swimmers that they have been stung by a jellyfish. The poisonous sea bladder is a giant among jellyfish. It drifts through cold waters. Its bell-shaped body may measure three feet (91.4 cm) across. Groups of stingers dangle among the tentacles.*

▼ GREAT BARRACUDA — Average length 4 ft (1.2 m)

2 *Great barracuda! Just the name of this fierce-looking fish (above) frightens some people. Barracudas seem to be curious about humans. They often follow divers. But they rarely attack. Even so, most diving instructors warn students to leave barracudas alone.*

3 *Yellow means caution for divers swimming near coral. Yellow fire coral can cause a painful sting. Many coral polyps have stinging cells. Usually, the poison in the cells is too weak to harm humans. But a fire coral sting can quickly ruin a diver's underwater adventure.*

4 *About 400 different kinds of cones live in the sea. A few can kill humans. One cone, named the geography because of the map-like patterns on its shell, lives in the South Pacific Ocean. It stabs enemies with a hollow tooth and forces in deadly poison.*

5 *Divers in the South Pacific Ocean and the Indian Ocean must look out for the stonefish. This fish hides among corals and rocks, concealed by its rough skin and mixed coloring. If stepped on, the stonefish forces deadly poison through spines on its back.*

59

Sleek hunter of the sea

A reef whitetip shark (right) patrols the sea. It moves like an armed submarine. Probably no other sea creature is so feared by humans as the shark. Yet sharks rarely bother swimmers.

Millions of people swim in the ocean every year. Sharks attack only about 40 or 50 of them. Perhaps half of those attacked survive.

A shark seeks wounded creatures as food. With its keen sense of smell, it sniffs out tiny amounts of blood in the water. So a diver carrying speared fish may attract a shark. Sharks also sense the jerky movements of an injured fish. Swimmers who spot a shark should swim to safety as calmly as possible.

Sharks are built for speed. They have no bones. Their bodies are supported by cartilage, which is lighter and more flexible than bone. Some sharks reach speeds of 43 miles (69 km) an hour. They also are powerful swimmers. They may dive to 12,000 feet (3,658 m).

Once people thought nothing could escape from a hungry shark. But the small fish below seems to be able to drive sharks away.

HUNGRY SHARKS *circle a fish called a Moses sole during an experiment. The sole produces a milky substance that poisons enemies. Scientists are trying to find out how the poison will affect enemies as large as sharks.*

SHARK JAWS LOCK *as the poison reaches them. Lids drop to protect the shark's eyes. The shark tries to back away. Scientists believe that sole may provide a valuable product: a material that drives sharks away from divers.*

REEF WHITETIP SHARK — Average length 8 ft (2.4 m)

SUNKEN TREASURE!

A team of scuba divers glides above the ocean floor. They are looking hard for something in the coral beneath them. One diver moves toward an open, sandy spot. The diver brushes away the sand and discovers a pile of gleaming gold coins and jewelry!

The story above may sound like a fairy tale. But people actually do find gold and other treasure on the ocean floor. Most of the treasure came from mines in the Americas. It was loaded aboard Spanish ships during the 16th, 17th, and 18th centuries. When the ships started to cross the stormy Caribbean on their way back to Spain, some hit reefs and sank.

Today, scientists and treasure hunters are locating some of this long-lost treasure. They find it by using modern tools and methods. One of their most important aids is research. Old books and papers can tell them where to begin. Then divers continue the search.

LOST AND FOUND. *This fortune in gold and jewels lay on the seafloor for more than 300 years. Divers recovered the treasure from the Maravillas, a Spanish ship that sank near the Bahama Islands in 1656.*

Pacific Ocean

Stormy paths to the New World

A fortune in silver and gold lay in the Americas. Spanish adventurers sailed thousands of miles to find it. Their wooden ships, armed galleons and smaller merchant vessels, followed trade routes across the Atlantic. The ships made use of the circular flow of ocean currents and winds to speed them on their way.

The galleons and some of the merchant vessels followed the route marked by a purple line on the map. They usually docked at Cartagena, in South America. Then they sailed on to Portobelo, a trading center. There, the crews swapped European tools, cloth, and other goods for South American products and silver. Returning to Cartagena, the ships took on American gold, pearls, leather, and emeralds.

Other Spanish ships took the route marked by the orange line. They sailed to Veracruz. These ships traded European goods for more New World products. Some took on silks and fine china from the Orient. Sometimes smaller ships went to ports off the main routes, such as Santo Domingo. Loaded with riches, all of the ships met in Havana, Cuba, for the return trip to Spain.

But dangerous coral reefs lay between the ships and the open seas. Sudden storms often swept across the Caribbean. Many ships never made it home. In 1641, disaster struck the *Concepción*. The ship sank with a fortune in treasure aboard. In 1715, a hurricane smashed into the Spanish treasure fleet. Ten ships went down. Hundreds of chests filled with silver and gold sank with them. Other ships met a similar end. Divers later recovered much of the cargo. But treasure worth millions of dollars still lies undiscovered along the Spanish trade routes.

VERACRUZ

DOOMED SHIP. *In Havana, Cuba, the Spanish ship* Atocha *awaits loading. Treasure chests, merchandise, and supplies line the wharf (below). Two days after it sailed, on September 6, 1622, a storm sent the* Atocha *to the bottom of the sea.*

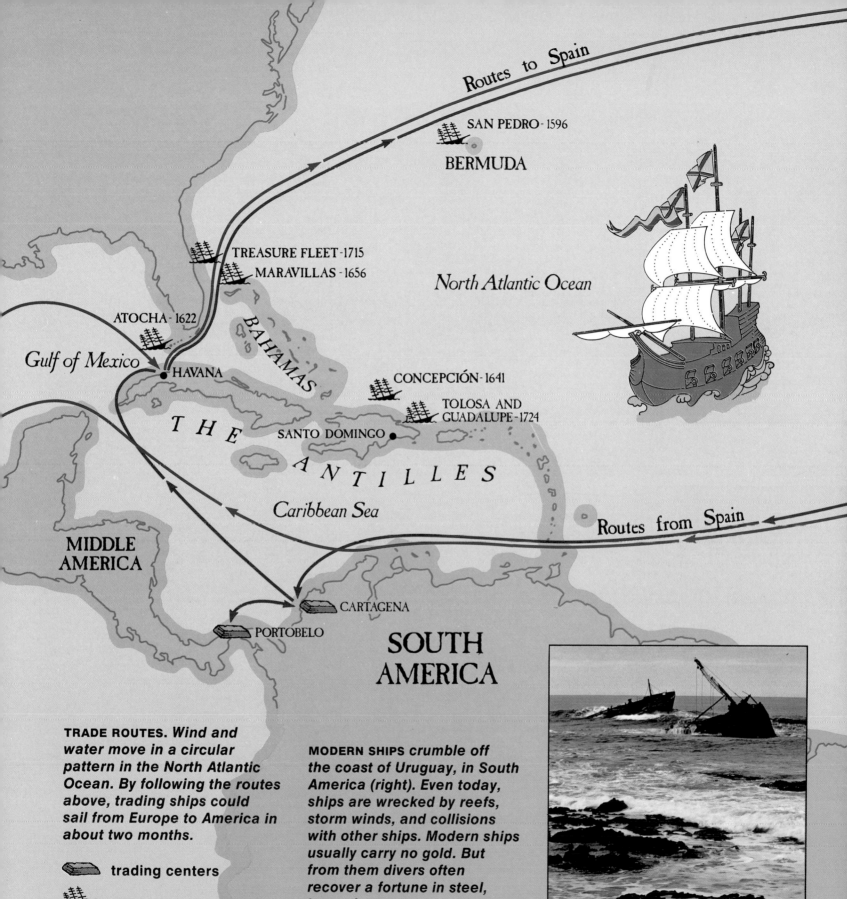

Routes to Spain

SAN PEDRO · 1596
BERMUDA

North Atlantic Ocean

TREASURE FLEET · 1715
MARAVILLAS · 1656

ATOCHA · 1622

BAHAMAS

Gulf of Mexico

HAVANA

CONCEPCIÓN · 1641

TOLOSA AND
GUADALUPE · 1724

THE ANTILLES

SANTO DOMINGO

Caribbean Sea

Routes from Spain

MIDDLE
AMERICA

CARTAGENA

PORTOBELO

SOUTH
AMERICA

TRADE ROUTES. *Wind and water move in a circular pattern in the North Atlantic Ocean. By following the routes above, trading ships could sail from Europe to America in about two months.*

🟫 trading centers

⛵ sites of major wrecks

MODERN SHIPS *crumble off the coast of Uruguay, in South America (right). Even today, ships are wrecked by reefs, storm winds, and collisions with other ships. Modern ships usually carry no gold. But from them divers often recover a fortune in steel, brass, instruments, and cargo.*

Finding and mapping a wreck site

Finding the pieces of a sunken ship is not as easy as most people think. Rocks may tear a sinking ship apart. Waves may scatter the pieces over the ocean floor. Marine worms usually eat away most of the exposed wood. Sand often covers all traces of the ship.

Discovering an ancient wreck in one piece is even harder. Sand or mud must settle over such a ship soon after it hits bottom. Otherwise, waves and worms usually damage it.

Treasure divers and archaeologists, scientists who study the past, often spend months searching for clues to the location of a wreck. They visit libraries and other places where old documents are kept. They search for firsthand reports, newspaper stories, and official records that describe a sinking.

Divers have many different ways of trying to find the actual wreck. They fly over the ocean looking for shapes, colors, or patterns that may indicate a man-made object in the water below. They scan the ocean floor with instruments that locate iron, or indicate buried objects.

Once a wreck is found, the slow, painstaking job of mapping the site begins. Divers record everything they find and carefully note the location of each object. If they do their work well, they often uncover enough clues to tell them where the ship came from, where it was going, and what happened during its last hours.

GETTING SET. *Divers prepare to explore a wreck site. They are trying to recover a Greek sailing ship. The ship sank off the island of Cyprus more than 2,200 years ago.*

WITH AN AIRLIFT, *or underwater vacuum cleaner, a diver clears mud from ancient wooden planks.*

PLASTIC PIPES *form a network, or grid, over the wreck site. The grid divides the site into sections. Divers draw or photograph the area within each section. That helps them keep track of what they find and where they find it.*

LUCKY FIND. *A diver scoops up coins scattered near broken pottery at a wreck site off Australia. She will carry the objects to the surface in the woven bag. Divers sometimes do not recognize silver coins. Salt water turns the coins black. It also may make them stick together in lumps.*

TREASURE DIVER *Dolores Fisher registers coins and jewelry (above) recovered from the* Atocha *wreck near Key West, Florida. State official Wilburn Cockrell lists each item. Florida keeps 25 percent of all treasure found in its waters.*

WITH A SMALL TOOL, *a diver scrapes mineral deposits from a 2,200-year-old wine jug recovered from the Mediterranean Sea (above). This pottery survived with little damage. Other materials don't last as well. Salt water weakens some metals, including iron. Sea creatures bore through wood— and even marble. Such materials often can be preserved by treating them with chemicals over many months.*

Preserving the past

Divers often spend years searching for a single wreck. They may also spend years bringing the cargo of that wreck safely to the surface. Even then the divers' work isn't finished.

Buried on the seafloor, some objects may survive for centuries. But once out of the water, they may be damaged by the air. As each item surfaces, workers remove any deposits left by the sea. Then they treat the object with chemicals and coat it with plastic or wax, to prevent further damage.

What happens to the treasure? In the United States, the government often allows divers to keep part of what they find. Most other countries claim objects found in their waters. Usually, scientists study the recovered objects. Then the objects may go to a museum where many people can enjoy them.

STURDY SOLDIER. *The small soldier (left) looks only a little damaged after spending more than 300 years in the sea. He went down with the* Lastdrager, *a 17th-century Dutch merchant ship that sank in 1653. In 1971, a treasure hunter found the wreckage off the northern coast of Scotland.*

An album of
TREASURES OF THE PAST

The golden objects on these pages shine as if they were fresh from a jewelry store. But each one rested on the ocean floor for more than 200 years. The chain, holding a whistle and a manicure set, may have belonged to an officer of a Spanish ship that was wrecked in 1622. The gold below, bearing treasury seals, was found near a 16th-century wreck. The Dutch coin went down with a merchant ship in 1737. The gold cross at far right probably was worn by a church official returning to Spain in 1596. All of these objects were recovered from the sea in the last 30 years.

▲ Gold chain and manicure set from the *Atocha*, lost in 1622

▲ Gold bullion from a 16th-century wreck off Bermuda

◀ Dutch coin recovered from the *Wendela*, sunk in 1737

In a museum in Santo Domingo, capital of the Dominican Republic, youngsters examine a different kind of treasure. European workers made the bottles, jewelry, and tableware for settlers in America. The cargo never reached the settlers. Two Spanish ships carrying these articles from Spain were wrecked in 1724. Whether made of precious gold or common clay, each object recovered from the sea helps give scientists and historians a more complete picture of the way people lived during the past.

▲ Household goods from the *Tolosa* and the *Guadalupe,* lost in 1724; on exhibit at the Casas Reales Museum, Santo Domingo, Dominican Republic; (from the left) Frederico, Francisco, and Genoveva Schad, 9, 8, and 8, and Carlos Borrell, 8

Gold cross, perhaps from the *San Pedro,* ▶ sunk in 1596 near Bermuda

71

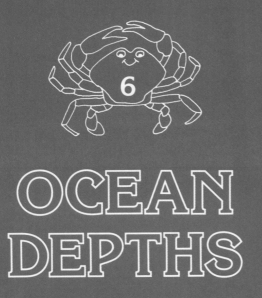

OCEAN DEPTHS

What would the ocean look like if all the water dried up? If you could explore an empty ocean floor, here is what you would see.

From the beach, you would find a wide plain sloping gently away from the shore. If you walked out onto the plain—sometimes for a short distance, sometimes for miles—you would find yourself on the top of a steep cliff. The ground would now lie miles below you. It would stretch farther than you could see.

This low-lying ground is the seafloor, the deepest part of the ocean. Shaped like a huge bowl, it holds 97 percent of the water in the sea.

The seafloor lies an average of 2.4 miles (3.8 km) below the surface. But it has trenches that reach seven miles (11 km) deep. It has mountains higher than any on land.

Aboard deep-diving craft like *Alvin* (right), a few people have visited parts of the seafloor. But scientists still know less about this huge area than they know about the moon.

LIGHTING UP *the dark ocean floor,* Alvin *hovers 8,500 feet (2,591 m) below the surface. The 24-foot sub helps scientists study the seafloor.*

Close-up look at a deep-diving sub

Alvin, a 15-year-old research submarine, has made more than 900 dives into the ocean depths. *Alvin*'s main job is to help scientists study the seafloor. But the sub has been involved in other adventures. In 1966, the U. S. Navy used it to help recover a nuclear bomb lost from a U. S. plane. In 1968, *Alvin* broke from its cables and sank in 5,000 feet (1,500 m) of water. The Navy raised it ten months later. Woods Hole Oceanographic Institution in Massachusetts operates *Alvin*. The Navy owns it.

MEET THE CLAW. *Dr. Robert D. Ballard (above) explains* Alvin's *claw to his sons, Douglas, 8, left, and Todd, 10. Dr. Ballard dives often in* Alvin *as part of his study of the seafloor. He is a geologist at Woods Hole Oceanographic Institution.*

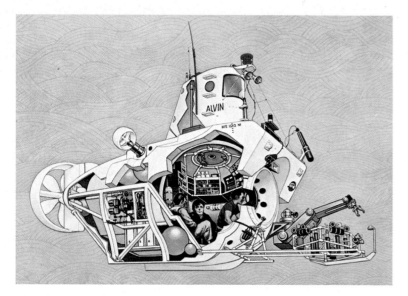

CLOSE QUARTERS. *Only a pilot and two passengers can fit in* Alvin's *working area (above). The space is less than seven feet wide. From inside, scientists control* Alvin's *claw. The claw collects things the scientists want to study. It puts the objects into a metal basket. Attached to* Alvin's *hull are lights, underwater cameras, and a tape recorder. A telephone links the sub to the* Lulu, *a boat that transports* Alvin *to its diving sites.*

AHOY, THERE. *Douglas looks through one of* Alvin's *five portholes (right). The sub runs on batteries. It can travel for as long as 10 hours at depths of more than 13,000 feet (4,000 m).*

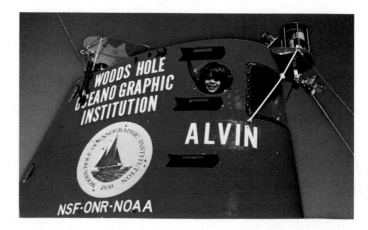

UNDERSEA TV! *Todd tunes in Douglas on Alvin's closed-circuit TV system. During a dive, scientists operate a TV camera that films the ocean around the sub. Back on dry land, they spend months studying information from the film.*

Exploring the rugged floor of the ocean

Until recently, people could only imagine what the ocean floor looked like. To find out how deep the water was, sailors used metal weights. They tied a weight to the end of a rope, then dropped the weight over the side of the ship to see how far it would sink.

Today, scientists know much more about how the ocean floor looks. They can even make maps and cutaway drawings like the one below. These drawings and maps are based on information gathered by instruments called echo sounders.

An echo sounder measures depth with sound. It sends sound waves to the seafloor. When the sound waves hit bottom, their echoes travel back to the surface. The echo sounder measures the time it takes for the waves and echoes to make the round trip. Then it translates the time into fathoms—a unit of length that equals six feet (1.8 m).

CONTINENTAL SHELF

The continental shelf is the outermost edge of a continent. It is a sloping, underwater plain. At its outer edge, the plain is covered by an average of 450 feet (137 m) of water. Rivers often cut channels down the slope and deposit sand and mud on the ocean floor below.

CONTINENTAL SLOPE

The outer edge of the continental shelf is called the continental slope. A steep cliff, the slope drops an average of 12,000 feet (3,658 m) to the seafloor.

ABYSSAL PLAIN

The flat area of the seafloor is called the abyssal plain. The abyssal plain is covered by a layer of mud, sand, and animal remains that have drifted down from higher levels over millions of years.

MID-OCEANIC RIDGE

A chain of mountains called the Mid-Oceanic Ridge runs along the center of the ocean. In all, this mountain chain twists for some 45,000 miles (72,464 km) around the earth.

RIFT VALLEY

Along the center of the Mid-Oceanic Ridge runs a steep-sided valley called a rift. Often, molten rock pushes up from its center.

SHRINKING CUP. *On one of* Alvin's *dives into the Cayman Trench, in the Caribbean Sea, crew members left a Styrofoam cup in the sub's observation tower. Unlike the cabin, this tower is not protected against the powerful pressure of the ocean depths. After a dive to 12,000 feet (3,658 m), the crew found out what ocean pressure can do: It squeezed the cup to about half the size of a normal cup (left). Such shrinkage actually occurs by the time the cup reaches 1,000 feet (304.8 m).*

SEAMOUNT

A seamount is an underwater mountain, usually built by a volcano. Some seamounts rise above the surface to become islands. But sometimes waves wear them away or they sink. Then they are again called seamounts.

CORAL ATOLL

A coral reef often forms around a volcanic island. Sometimes the island sinks into the sea, and the coral reef continues to grow. The remaining coral ring is called an atoll.

VOLCANO

Volcanoes often erupt on the seafloor. They build mountains. When the mountains grow high enough to break through the surface of the sea, they become islands, such as those of the Hawaiian chain. One Hawaiian island rises more than 30,000 feet (9,120 m) from the ocean floor!

TRENCH

Long, narrow valleys called trenches cut through the seafloor in some places. These trenches hold the deepest parts of the ocean. Some trenches are more than 34,000 feet (10,336 m) deep.

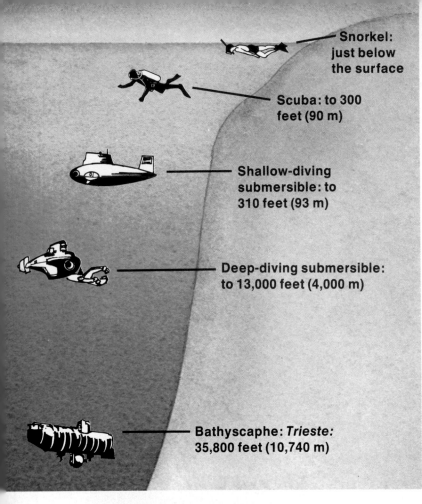

Snorkel: just below the surface

Scuba: to 300 feet (90 m)

Shallow-diving submersible: to 310 feet (93 m)

Deep-diving submersible: to 13,000 feet (4,000 m)

Bathyscaphe: *Trieste*: 35,800 feet (10,740 m)

Submersibles: Windows on a watery world

People know so little about the seafloor because only recently have they had the equipment to go there. Fifty years ago, they could dive only as deep as their breath could take them, or as far as a tube from the surface could reach.

Today, scientists visit the seafloor in submersibles. A submersible is a submarine, a ship that travels underwater. It has an engine, and a shell strong enough to withstand the tons of water pressure at the ocean bottom. Inside, the cabin air pressure stays the same as the air pressure at the surface of the sea.

In the future, submersibles may provide answers to many of the mysteries of the sea.

REACHING THE DEEP. *With the right kind of gear, people can go almost anywhere in the sea. The painting at left shows some of the undersea vessels and breathing gear in use today. It also shows how deep each can operate safely.*

SEA MONSTER? *No, it's* Jim, *a one-person submersible. In it, a diver can work 1,500 feet (450 m) down. Jim was named after the diver who first tested it.*

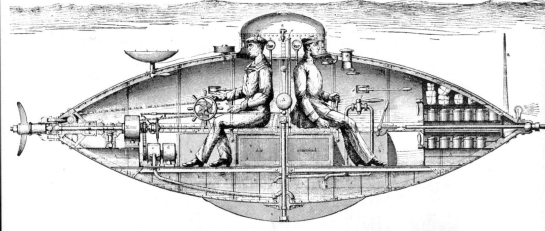

EARLY SUBMARINE. *People tried for centuries to build a ship that could travel underwater. They wanted to use it during times of war. In 1887, the French navy tried out a two-man sub (above). But it was too small and too slow for the navy to use. During World War I, submarines were built that could move at depths of 200 feet (60 m). By World War II, they reached twice that depth. Modern subs can dive to more than 4,000 feet (1,200 m). They also can go around the world without coming to the surface.*

PERRY CUBMARINE 8 can carry two people down to 800 feet (240 m). A diving service uses this mini-sub to build and repair oil pipelines.

Homemade mini-sub goes to sea

"My friend Jay laughed at me when I said we should build a submarine," says Marshall Simmons, of Vista, California. "Then I showed him my plans. We started building three months later."

Marshall and Jay Welch worked in a metal shop owned by Marshall's father. A year later, they pulled their battery-operated sub, the *Nemo,* into the water. Hatches leaked, and the electricity failed. But the builders of the *Nemo* decided to keep working until the one-ton craft was seaworthy. Why did they build the *Nemo*? "Just for fun," says Marshall.

FINAL CHECK. *Marshall Simmons and Jay Welch (above), of Vista, California, check out their one-person sub, the* Nemo. *The two 18-year-olds spent about 1,000 hours building the sub.*

TEST DIVE. *As his brother, Mitchell, steadies the sub, Marshall prepares to submerge (above). Marshall built a diving helmet before he began the* Nemo. *"I'm always building something," he says.*

LAUNCH TIME! *A crowd gathers as Marshall and Jay launch the* Nemo *at Oceanside (left). They used a trailer to move the sub into the water.*

LOCKING UP. *Marshall pulls down the hatch (left) just before the* Nemo *dives under the water (right). To make the sub dive, Marshall pumps water into tanks in the ship's body. To bring the sub to the surface, he pumps the water out again.*

81

▲ MEDUSA: Average length 5 in (12.7 cm)

An album of
DEEP-SEA CREATURES

Sunlight never reaches the deepest parts of the ocean. At about 3,000 feet (900 m), total darkness begins. In the deepest regions, temperatures stay near freezing. The water pressure there is powerful enough to squeeze and shrink wood until it is half its original size. This pressure can crush an unprotected human being.

Once people thought nothing could live at the bottom of the sea. Then, about 100 years ago, scientists developed ways of dragging heavy nets across the seafloor. The nets scooped up a variety of familiar animals, such as crabs and worms. They also brought up strange-looking creatures like the medusa, the five-inch-long (13 cm) jellyfish at left.

In 1960, the *Trieste*, a submersible called a bathyscaphe, reached the bottom of the deepest trench yet discovered in the ocean. Even at this depth, 35,817 feet (10,917 m), the crew found life. A fish swam by the lighted porthole.

Aboard submersibles, scientists still have explored only a small area of the seafloor. But the more they probe the sea, the more life they discover in this harsh world.

Dark and cold, the ocean depths might seem to be a lifeless place. Plants do not grow in total darkness. But many kinds of animals can live in the dark. Some, like shrimps and jellyfish, stay far below the surface during the day. At night, they come to the surface to feed on plankton. Other animals, such as worms, starfish, and sea urchins, usually stay on the bottom. They eat the remains of plants and animals that drift slowly down from higher levels.

Scientists once thought that the seafloor was a silent place. But microphones lowered into the sea pick up many sounds. They record a mixture of squeaks, moans, coughs, squeals, whistles, and clicks. Some creatures seem to use sounds to find mates. Others may locate the bottom by making sounds and judging how long it takes for the echoes to return.

Scientists also have learned that the bottom of the ocean is not totally dark. Some creatures produce their own light. They make it from chemicals in their bodies. The light may help the animals find food. It also may confuse their enemies or attract others of their kind.

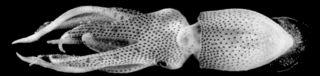

▲ RED SHRIMP: Average length 3.5 in (8.9 cm)

▲ SQUID: Average length 2 in (5 cm)

CREATURES OF THE DEEP. *Both the red shrimp (above) and the squid (left) live in deep water during the day. There, the darkness helps protect them from hungry enemies. At night they swim to the surface and feed on plankton. Squids also eat fish, shrimps, and other squids. In turn, the squids are hunted by fish such as the fangtooth and hatchet fish.*

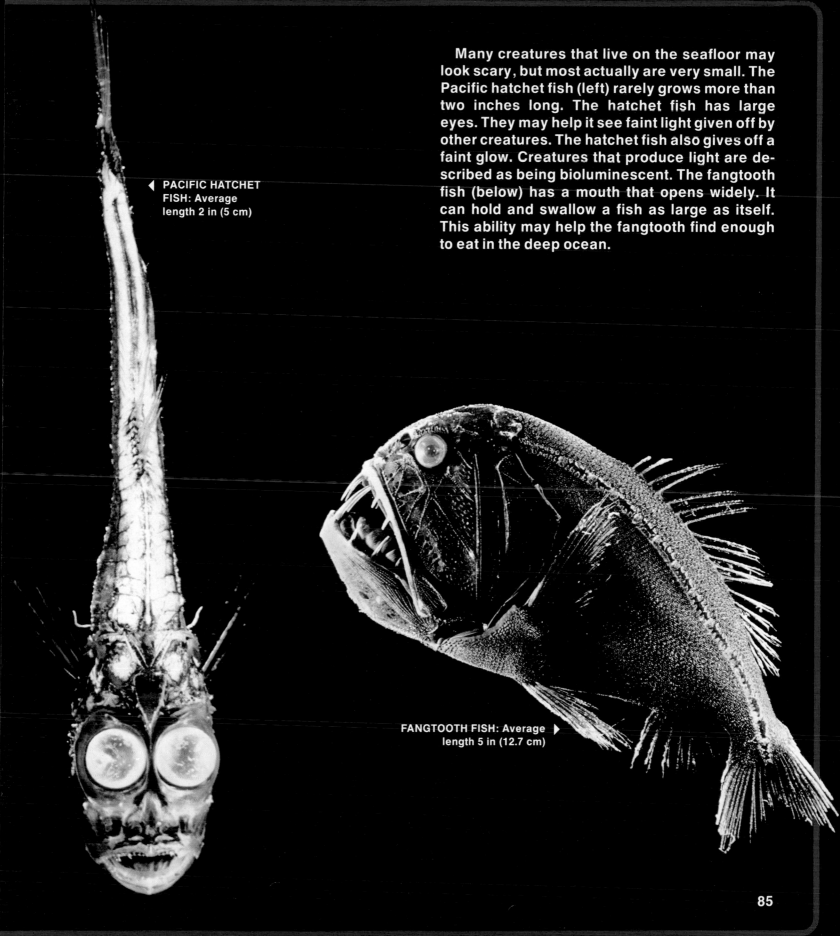

Many creatures that live on the seafloor may look scary, but most actually are very small. The Pacific hatchet fish (left) rarely grows more than two inches long. The hatchet fish has large eyes. They may help it see faint light given off by other creatures. The hatchet fish also gives off a faint glow. Creatures that produce light are described as being bioluminescent. The fangtooth fish (below) has a mouth that opens widely. It can hold and swallow a fish as large as itself. This ability may help the fangtooth find enough to eat in the deep ocean.

◀ PACIFIC HATCHET FISH: Average length 2 in (5 cm)

FANGTOOTH FISH: Average ▶ length 5 in (12.7 cm)

Right at home on the seafloor

In 1963, scientists began to live and work under the sea. Their first stay on the seafloor was on Starfish House, the underwater habitat below.

A habitat is a place that keeps people safe in unusual surroundings. Starfish House is like an underwater apartment. It has sleeping quarters and a kitchen. The air pressure inside is kept equal to the water pressure outside. Because the pressures are equal, divers have to go through decompression only at the end of their stay. Telephones link the habitat with the ships on the surface that supply it with air and food.

The U. S. Navy began testing habitats called Sealabs in 1964. Aboard the Sealabs, divers experimented with cameras and recorded sounds. They also tried breathing different mixtures of oxygen and other gases. A trained dolphin named Tuffy carried mail down from the surface.

Tektite II, a habitat sponsored by scientific groups, rested on a reef near the Virgin Islands for seven months during 1969 and 1970. Scientists, engineers, and doctors stayed there for as long as 60 days. Soon people may live under the sea for even longer periods of time.

STARFISH HOUSE *rests on the bottom of the Red Sea. Five divers lived on board for a month. They were beneath 36 feet (11 m) of water.*

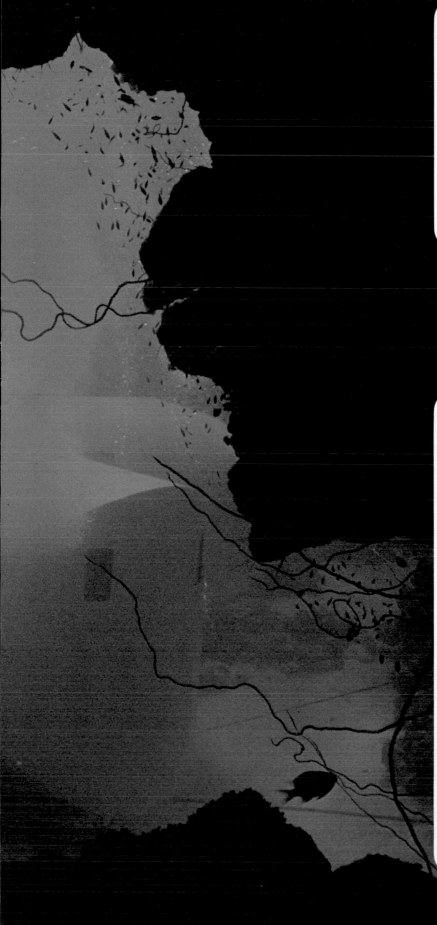

UNDERSEA DINNER. *Scientists share a meal 50 feet (15 m) under the surface (above). The five-woman team lived for two weeks in Tektite II.*

WINDOW ON THE SEA. *Diver André Folco ignores curious visitors outside Starfish House (below). He sits in the habitat's living room.*

MINIATURE OCEANS

7

As eager as a puppy, Shamu, a 22-foot killer whale, slides up on a poolside platform to greet a trainer. Shamu performs each day for thousands of visitors. Shamu lives at Sea World of San Diego, in California.

Most people never have a chance to snorkel or scuba dive. Fewer still will explore the ocean in a mini-sub. For them, an oceanarium like Sea World provides a close-up look at many creatures they would never see anywhere else.

A group of scientists also studies at Sea World. The scientists work for Hubbs-Sea World Research Institute. Often they travel to distant places to observe wild animals in natural surroundings. But the scientists often can't follow a sea creature into the ocean depths. So they observe the animal at the oceanarium.

These scientists are studying subjects such as pollution, and the damage it does to life in the oceans. Their work is important. It may help some creatures survive.

WHALE OF A SHOW. *Shamu, an 8,000-pound (3,600 kg) killer whale, performs at Sea World of San Diego, in California.*

FLYING WHALE. *Trainers at Sea World of Ohio, in Aurora, guide Shamu into a tank (left). After wintering in San Diego, some whales go by plane to Ohio in padded containers.*

WANDA THE WALRUS *(right) often sprays water on visitors to Sea World of San Diego. Teddy Lowe, 9, of Pacific Palisades, California, left, and Sherri and William Baxter, 9 and 8, of Wayzata, Minnesota, pass her very carefully.*

Enjoying the show at an oceanarium

Crowds at Sea World love to see Shamu perform. Sea World trainers work with ten killer whales. Each whale is known as Shamu when it performs for audiences. Killer whales are very smart. They learn quickly. As a reward for obeying a trainer's command, they receive food, a pat on the head, or a play period. Trainers say the whales seem to love having their backs rubbed.

Killer whales earned their name because of the way they hunt in the wild. Traveling in packs, they surround and attack seals, walruses, sea otters, and smaller whales. But they are gentle with humans.

Wild killer whales are protected by law. Sea World officials must have permission from the federal government to keep them. The whales are collected in nets. Then they are packed in cradles padded with damp foam rubber for the trip to San Diego. Sea World also has branches in Ohio and Florida.

SHAMU GLIDES OVER A ROPE *while performing at Sea World of San Diego (right). In the wild, killer whales can swim as fast as 30 miles (48 km) an hour. They often slide onto blocks of ice to capture walruses or seals. Like some other whales, killer whales may communicate with sounds.*

90

WEIGHING IN. *At Sea World of San Diego, Kim Mikula weighs an Adélie penguin (left). Another penguin waits its turn. Sea World keeps a colony of these creatures for study. In the wild, Adélies live in Antarctica.*

SEA LIONS *greet animal care expert Dee Gross (right). The Hubbs-Sea World staff often cares for orphaned or ill wild creatures. Many of them are returned to the wild. Some are placed in zoos or other exhibits.*

YELLOWTAILS GLIDE *beyond clear walls at the Steinhart Aquarium, in San Francisco, California.*

Finding worlds of life at an aquarium

Aquariums, like oceanariums, display ocean creatures in huge tanks, often with lifelike settings. Visitors to the Steinhart Aquarium, in San Francisco, California, can see about 800 different kinds of creatures. This collection has the greatest variety of any in the world.

Ocean water keeps the animals alive and healthy. The water circulates through 190 aquarium tanks. The tanks range in size from 5 to 100,000 gallons (19-378,500 l). Biologists feed the creatures food much like the food they would eat in the wild. A team of young volunteers helps clean the tanks and feed the fish. The Steinhart Aquarium is part of the California Academy of Sciences.

YOUNG LECTURERS. *Elizabeth Mead, holding a microphone, and Paul Lewis, 13, in a yellow apron, point out residents in a tide-pool exhibit. Elizabeth, Paul, and other volunteers spend Saturdays working at the Steinhart Aquarium.*

PREPARING DINNER. *Steinhart volunteer Llisa Demetrios, 12, chops fish (left). Gabrielle Rudenko, also 12, will feed a pan of shrimplike krill, whole mackerel, and squid to fish in the aquarium tanks. "We do a lot of jobs here," says Gabrielle. "I like feeding fish the best."*

LUNCH, ULYSSES? *Ulysses the grouper is a special friend of Gabrielle (above). "I almost play with him," she says. "I put a fish in his mouth and often he drops it. Then he goes off to hide. I have to pick up his food and wave it in front of him again. Ulysses acts as if he's doing me a favor by eating it." Ulysses is 21 years old, and measures about three feet (91.4 cm) long. He eats three mackerel a day. "Feeding the fish isn't hard," says Gabrielle. "I always wear old clothes and sneakers. With this job, I get pretty wet."*

WORKING WITH CARE. *Rick Giron, 13, pulls a young leopard shark from an aquarium tank (left). Before moving it to a new display tank, he checks the fish's eyes for possible damage. Sometimes, fish in a tank attack each other. Rick helps in an area devoted to American saltwater fishes. He works with the aquarium's senior biologist. Rick hopes to become a biologist himself someday. "I'm very interested in sea life," he says. "In fact, I have about 20 tanks at home."*

93

Setting up a saltwater aquarium

Scientists have learned much about living creatures by studying sea life at aquariums and oceanariums. Their findings enable people to have saltwater aquariums in their homes.

Keeping up an aquarium is a big responsibility. Like all pets, fish need attention. Caring for them takes about an hour a week. You must follow certain rules to keep each fish healthy. Before you set up a saltwater aquarium, read books about the fish you plan to include in it.

An aquarium probably will be expensive. A fully equipped saltwater tank costs at least $50. Saltwater fish cost $5 to $20 apiece or more. To have room for a variety of fish, experts suggest using a tank holding at least 20 gallons (75.7 l) of water. Use an all-glass tank. Some metals form harmful chemicals when salt water touches them. Water collected from the ocean may be polluted. It also may contain things poisonous to your fish. Dry saltwater mixes are better. You add the mix to tap water, following the instructions on the package.

Starting at the bottom, Mike Moore puts part of an underwater filter into a glass tank. He will cover the filter with gravel. The filter and gravel clean the water. Attached to the filter is a pump. The pump mixes air with the water and causes it to circulate. As the water goes through the filter and gravel, wastes made by fish are strained out.

MIKE AT WORK. *Sixteen-year-old Mike Moore (left) of Del Mar, California, is a volunteer at Scripps Institution of Oceanography, in La Jolla. Mike does many jobs there. One is to test the water used in the tanks. Here, he records the amount of nitrogen in samples of water. Too much nitrogen can harm the fish. "Fish can get the bends just as humans can," he says. Mike also carries out experiments. Last year, he worked out a way to keep dolphins from being caught in fishing nets. Government officials are checking into his plan.*

Almost finished, Mike checks to see if all the equipment works (right). He has placed an "airstone" in the center of the tank. Air pumped through the airstone keeps the water moving and adds oxygen to the water. Other tubes circulate the water through an outside filter. Mike now will install a hydrometer, an instrument for measuring salt in the water. Fish cannot live in water that contains too little or too much salt. Then he will add decorations, such as pieces of coral.

Mike spreads gravel over the filter (above). He uses a kind of stone called dolomite. To make sure the dolomite is free of dust, Mike has rinsed it with clear water. If dust clogs the gills of a fish, the fish may die.

After preparing a saltwater mix, Mike begins to fill the tank (above). To keep from stirring up the gravel, he puts a dish in the tank. Then he fills the dish with a hose and lets the water flow over the rim.

Mike sets up a thermometer in the tank (above). Some saltwater fish can live only in warm water. To keep the temperature at a healthful 75° F (23.9° C), Mike has clipped a heater in the corner of the tank.

Selecting your pets

Let your tank sit for six to eight days. Be sure all of the equipment works properly. Then you can begin to buy your fish. At first choose strong, inexpensive fish, such as the sergeant major or clown fish.

Choose every fish carefully. Look for a fish that swims well and looks alert. Its colors should be bright. Its body and fins should be in good condition. Ask the dealer to feed the fish. If a fish won't eat in the store, it may not eat in your tank. Before buying any fish, find out whether it might harm other fish you plan to include in your tank.

Don't try to fill your tank with fish all at once. Buy only a few fish at a time. Let them become accustomed to living together before adding more.

CATCHING A CLOWN. *Aquarium shop owner Eve Moore nets a clown fish (upper left) for Steven, left, and Adam Rice, 12 and 11, of North Miami Beach, Florida. Before making their selection, the boys found out what kind of fish would get along with the fish already in the tank they own.*

FINDING OUT THE FACTS. *Mrs. Moore shows Steven and Adam some books that explain how to care for their new pet (left). To ensure a healthy life for the clown fish, the boys must know what it eats and how much light and space it requires.*

WELCOME HOME! *Steven and Adam lower the bag containing the clown fish into their tank (above). This allows the fish to adjust slowly to the temperature of its new home. Then they will pour some water out of the bag and replace it with water from the tank. They repeat this every 15 minutes for several hours. When the fish has become used to the new water, they will release it in the tank.*

FEEDING TIME. *Steven hand-feeds a French angelfish, which lives in another of his tanks (left). The boys captured the angelfish off Miami Beach.*

97

HOME, SWEET HOME. *Only certain kinds of fish can survive in the same tank. In the aquarium on these pages, a flame surgeonfish hides among coral. Two yellow surgeons and a smooth unicorn fish drift nearby. A tank in which different kinds of fish live peacefully together is called a community tank.*

CLOWN FISH AND SEA ANEMONES *form partnerships. The clown fish swim and feed among the anemones' tentacles. When these creatures live in a tank like the one above, the fish must have plenty of space, and enough anemones to go around. Otherwise, the fish may fight. Before selecting such creatures, an aquarium owner should know the needs of each one.*

SETTING SUN *colors a beach where two youngsters stop to examine a starfish.*

no one has found easy and inexpensive ways to separate the minerals from the water.

Our oceans also are a rich source of food. This food is badly needed because the land does not provide enough food for the growing number of people who live on the earth today. Yet only a small part of the food people eat comes from the sea.

Scientists are looking for ways to harvest and use more fish, shellfish, and seaweeds.

Many scientists fear that pollution could ruin the sea as a source of food. Insecticides wash down from the land and settle in the water. Factory wastes dumped into rivers end up in the oceans. Raw sewage drains into the sea from some cities and towns. Radioactive wastes are dropped into the ocean depths. Shipping accidents cause oil spills that kill wildlife and damage beaches.

As a result of such pollution, many ocean animals die. Other creatures, although they don't become sick, carry man-made poisons in their bodies. When larger animals, including humans, eat a poisoned animal, they may become ill.

Solutions to the problem of pollution will not be easy to find, nor will they be popular with everyone. But most people agree that the oceans must remain healthy if life is to continue on the earth.

Saving our oceans

Approaching the earth, a visitor from another planet would see a bright, sea-blue ball spinning in black space.

Because so much of the earth is covered by water, the visitor might expect to find people living in the oceans. But people don't live there, of course. And not until about a century ago did they begin to explore the ocean depths.

Since then, scientists and divers have discovered much about the undersea world. They have found, for example, that sea water is rich in minerals. In most cases, however,

Pronunciation Guide

CHAPTER 1

neap	(neep)
centrifugal	(sen-TRIFF-uh-gul)

CHAPTER 2

La Jolla	(LA HOY-uh)
chiton	(KYE-tun)
opaleye	(OH-pul-eye)
algae	(AL-jee)
anemone	(uh-NEM-uh-nee)
coquina	(koe-KEE-nuh)
bivalve	(BYE-valve)
grunion	(GRUNN-yun)

CHAPTER 3

polyp	(POLL-ip)
gorgonian	(gor-GO-nee-un)
wrasse	(rass)
Dendronephthya	(den-dro-NEFF-thee-uh)
Leptastrea purpurea	(lep-TASS-tree-uh pur-pur-EE-uh)
nudibranch	(NOOD-uh-brank)
polychaete	(POLL-ee-keet)
harlequin	(HAR-lih-kin)

CHAPTER 4

nitrogen	(NYE-truh-jen)
hydrozoan	(hye-druh-ZOH-un)
barracuda	(bare-ruh-KOO-duh)

CHAPTER 5

Maravillas	(mar-uh-VEE-yus)
galleon	(GAL-ee-un)
Cartagena	(car-tuh-HAY-nuh)
Veracruz	(veh-ruh-KROOZE)
Caribbean	(care-uh-BEE-un) or (kuh-RIB-ee-un)
Concepción	(cun-sep-see-OHN)
Atocha	(uh-TOE-chuh)
Mediterranean	(med-ih-tur-RANE-ee-un)
Tolosa	(toh-LOW-sah)
Guadalupe	(gwah-duh-LOO-pay)
Uruguay	(OOR-uh-gwye)
archaeologist	(ar-kee-AH-luh-jist)
Cyprus	(SYE-pruss)
Lastdrager	(LASS-drag-er)
Reales	(ray-AH-les)

CHAPTER 6

atoll	(AT-tall)
abyssal	(uh-BISS-ul)
bathyscaphe	(BATH-ih-skaff)
submersible	(sub-MURR-sih-bul)
medusa	(mih-DOO-sah)
Trieste	(tree-EST)
bioluminescent	(bye-oh-loo-mih-NESS-ent)

CHAPTER 7

oceanarium	(oh-shun-AIR-ee-um)
dolomite	(DOE-luh-mite)
hydrometer	(hye-DROM-ih-ter)

Additional Reading

Readers may want to check the National Geographic Index in a school or public library for related articles, and to refer to the following books:

General: Carson, Rachel. *The Sea Around Us.* (N.Y.: Golden Press, 1958.) Jensen, Albert. *Wildlife of the Oceans.* (N.Y.: Harry N. Abrams, 1979.) Limburg, Peter R., and James B. Sweeney. *102 Questions and Answers About the Sea.* (N.Y.: Julian Messner, 1975.) Williams, Jerome. *Oceanography.* (N.Y.: Franklin Watts, Inc., 1972.)

Chapter 1: Clemons, Elizabeth. *Waves, Tides, and Currents.* (N.Y.: Alfred A. Knopf, 1967.) Engel, Leonard. *The Sea.* (N.Y.: Time, Inc., 1967.)

Chapter 2: Amos, William H. *The Life of the Seashore.* (N.Y.: McGraw-Hill, 1966.) Kohn, Bernice. *The Beachcomber's Book.* (N.Y.: Puffin Books, 1970.) List, Ilka K. *Questions and Answers about Seashore Life.* (N.Y.: Four Winds Press, 1970.) Silverberg, Robert. *The World Within the Tide Pool.* (N.Y.: Weybright & Talley, 1972.)

Chapter 3: Darling, Lois and Louis. *Coral Reefs.* (Cleveland: The World Publishing Co., 1963.) Tinker, Gene and Barbara. *Let's Learn to Snorkel.* (N.Y.: Walker and Co., 1969.) Zim, Herbert S. *Corals.* (N.Y.: William Morrow and Co., 1966.)

Chapter 4: National Geographic Society. *Undersea Treasures.* (Washington, D. C.: 1974.) The National Association of Skin Diving Schools. *Safe Scuba.* (Long Beach, California: 1975.)

Chapter 5: National Geographic Society. *Secrets from the Past.* (Washington, D. C., 1979.) Marx, Robert F. *The Underwater Dig.* (N.Y.: Henry Z. Walck, Inc., 1975.)

Chapter 6: Barton, Robert. *Atlas of the Sea.* (N.Y.: The John Day Co., 1974.) Berger, Melvin. *Oceanography Lab.* (N.Y.: John Day Co., 1973.) Cox, Donald W. *Explorers of the Deep.* (Maplewood, N.J.: Hammond, Inc., 1968.) McFall, Christie. *Underwater Continent: The Continental Shelves.* (N.Y.: Dodd, Mead & Co., 1975.) Ross, Frank, Jr. *Undersea Vehicles and Habitats.* (N.Y.: Thomas Crowell, 1970.)

Chapter 7: McCoy, J. J. *A Sea of Troubles.* (N.Y.: The Seabury Press, 1975.) Sarnoff, Jane, and Reynold Ruffins. *A Great Aquarium Book.* (N.Y.: Charles Scribner's Sons, 1977.)

Index

Bold type refers to illustrations; regular type refers to text.

Consultants

Nancy Kaufman, Fishery Resources, U. S. Fish and Wildlife Service, *Chief Consultant*
Judith M. Hobart, *Educational Consultant*
Dr. Nicholas L. Long, *Consulting Psychologist*
The Special Publications and School Services Division is grateful to the individuals, organizations, and agencies named or quoted in the text and to those cited here for their generous assistance: Smithsonian Institution; Shane Anderson, Marine Science Institute, University of California, Santa Barbara; Captain Tracy Bowden; Dr. Eugenie Clark, Department of Zoology, University of Maryland; Donald Dewey, editor *Freshwater and Marine Aquarium*; Dr. John D. Donnelly, Arnold Sharp, both Woods Hole Oceanographic Institution; Dr. Frederick van Doorninck, Institute of Nautical Archaeology; Dr. Jack Engle, Greg Hageman, both Catalina Marine Science Center; Dr. John McCosker, Director, Steinhart Aquarium, California Academy of Sciences; Larry McGrath, Perry Oceanographics, Inc., Riviera Beach, Florida; Robert Marx; Barbara Moore, Educational Programs Office, Scripps Institution of Oceanography; Mendel Peterson; Craig Phillips, National Aquarium; Dr. Marie Tharp, Lamont Daugherty Company, Palisades, New York; Ed Wardwell, Oceaneering International, Santa Barbara, California.

Far-out Fun: *Front cover:* Ed Robinson, photograph; Paul M. Breeden, art; *pages 2-22:* Sue Levin; *page 23:* Joseph H. Bailey, NGS; *Back cover:* Pat Morris ARDEA/London (top left); Stephen C. Earley (top center, bottom left); Marty Snyderman (top right); Howard Hall (bottom center); Geri Murphy (bottom right).

Composition for *The Mysterious Undersea World* by National Geographic's Photographic Services, Carl M. Shrader, Chief; Lawrence F. Ludwig, Assistant Chief. Printed and bound by Holladay-Tyler Printing Corp., Rockville, Md. Color separations by Graphic South, Charlotte, N.C.; Progressive Color Corp., Rockville, Md.; The J. Wm. Reed Co., Alexandria, Va.; *Far-out Fun,* dry transfers produced by Dennison Manufacturing Co., Framingham, Mass.

Library of Congress CIP Data
Cook, Jan Leslie.
  The mysterious undersea world.
  (Books for world explorers)
  Bibliography: p.   Includes index
  SUMMARY: Introduces the ocean and its movements, marine animals and plants, sunken treasure, submersibles, aquariums, and oceanariums.
  1. Ocean—Juvenile literature. 2. Marine biology—Juvenile literature.
  [1. Ocean. 2. Marine biology] I. Title. II. Series. GC21.5.C66 551.4'6
79-1791   ISBN 0-87044-317-8

ILLUSTRATIONS CREDITS: Ed Robinson (cover); Chuck Nicklin/Woodfin Camp (1); Jonathan Blair (2-3, poster); Viviane Y. Silverman, NGS (chapter opener art).

CHAPTER 1: Bob Barbour/Surfing Magazine (4-5); Jon Brenneis (6-7); Doug M. Wilson (7 bottom left); Lisa Biganzoli, NGS (7 right, 9 center both); Albert Moldvay (8); Tom Myers (9 top both).

CHAPTER 2: Ron Church (10-11); Albert Moldvay (12, 13 left both, 22-23 all); Neil McDaniel (13 right); Lloyd K. Townsend (14); Ed Robinson (15 top); Thomas Cowell (15 left, 16 top, 17 top right, 20-21); Jack Drake/Black Star (16 bottom); Jeff Rotman (17 top left); Al Lowry, Nat'l Audubon Society/PR (17 bottom); Al Giddings—Ocean Films/Ocean Trust (18); Howard Hall (18 inset, 21 left inset); Bianca Lavies, NGS (19 top left, bottom); Charles E. Herron, NGS (19 top right); ANIMALS ANIMALS/Zig Leszczynski (20 left inset); James H. Carmichael Jr., Nat'l Audubon Society/PR (20 right inset); Lowell Georgia (21 right inset); Ben Cropp (24-25 top); Robert F. Sisson, NGS (24 bottom both); Roger T. Hanlon (25 top right); Stephen C. Earley (25 bottom right).

CHAPTER 3: Stephen C. Earley (26-31 all except 29 top left, 36, 37 center, 42 left, 45 bottom); Charles W. Berry, NGS (29 top left); Valerie Taylor/ARDEA London (32-33); Jeff Rotman (34 left); Scott Johnson (34-35 bottom, 39 right center inset, 43); Susan Sanford (35 top left); Ron & Valerie Taylor/ARDEA London (35 top right); Jonathan Blair (35 bottom right); ANIMALS ANIMALS/Zig Leszczynski (36 inset, 39 bottom left, top right insets, 44 bottom); Roger T. Hanlon (37 bottom); ANIMALS ANIMALS/Carl Roessler (38-39, 39 bottom right inset, 40, 41 bottom right); Ben Cropp (39 top left inset); David Doubilet (39 center inset, 42 top, 44 top); Neil McDaniel (40-41 bottom, 41 top right); Ron Taylor/ARDEA London (41 top left); Howard Hall (42 bottom right); Thomas Cowell (45 top); Ed Robinson (45 center right).

CHAPTER 4: David Doubilet (46-47, 56-57, 57 top right, 60 both); Jonathan Blair (48-53 all except 49 bottom and 53 left); 19th-century engraving from Hachette (49 bottom); George Marler (53 left, 59 top center left); Geri Murphy (54-55, 59 right); John E. Randall (57 bottom right); Thomas Cowell (58 left); Bianca Lavies, NGS (58 top right); Doug Wallin (58 bottom right); Neil McDaniel (59 top left); Valerie Taylor/ARDEA London (59 bottom center left); ANIMALS ANIMALS/Zig Leszczynski (59 bottom left); Howard Hall (60-61).

CHAPTER 5: David L. Arnold, NGS, Seafinders, Inc., Tulsa, Oklahoma (62-63); Charles W. Berry, NGS & Alfred Zebarth, NGS (64-65); Noel Sickles (64 bottom); Bruce Dale, NGS (65 bottom); Bates Littlehales, NGS (66-67 all, 69 top left, bottom center, 70 bottom center); Ben Cropp (68); Otis Imboden, NGS (69 top right); Emory Kristof, NGS (70 left); Robert S. Patton, NGS (70 top right); Jonathan Blair, Caribe Salvage S.A. (71 left); Emory Kristof, NGS, courtesy Govt. of Bermuda (71 right).

CHAPTER 6: Emory Kristof, NGS & Alvin M. Chandler, NGS (72-73); Davis Meltzer (74 left); Emory Kristof, NGS (74 right both, 75, 77); Lloyd K. Townsend (76-77); Charles W. Berry, NGS (78 top); Ira Block (78 bottom left); Culver Pictures, Inc. (78 bottom right); Andy Pruna (79); Albert Moldvay (80-81 all); Langdon B. Quetin (82-85 all); Robert B. Goodman, NGS (86-87, 87 bottom inset); Flip Schulke/Black Star (87 top inset).

CHAPTER 7: Stephen C. Earley (88-91 all except 90 top left, 94 bottom, 96-97 all); Steven R. Szerdy, Sea World, Aurora, Ohio (90 top left); Steinhart Aquarium, California Academy of Science—Rob Super (92 top); Albert Moldvay (92 bottom, 93-95 all except art and 94 bottom, 98-99, 100); Sue Levin (94-95 art); ANIMALS ANIMALS/Zig Leszczynski (99 inset).

The Mysterious Undersea World
by Jan Leslie Cook

PUBLISHED BY
THE NATIONAL GEOGRAPHIC SOCIETY

Robert E. Doyle, *President*
Melvin M. Payne, *Chairman of the Board*
Gilbert M. Grosvenor, *Editor*
Melville Bell Grosvenor, *Editor Emeritus*

PREPARED BY THE SPECIAL PUBLICATIONS
AND SCHOOL SERVICES DIVISION
Robert L. Breeden, *Director*
Donald J. Crump, *Associate Director*
Philip B. Silcott, *Assistant Director*

Staff for Books for WORLD Explorers Series: Ralph Gray, *Editor;* Pat Robbins, *Managing Editor;* Ursula Perrin Vosseler, *Art Director*

Staff for this Book:
Margaret McKelway, *Managing Editor*
Charles E. Herron, *Picture Editor*
Viviane Y. Silverman, *Designer*
Joan Tapper, Merrill Windsor, *Consulting Editors;* Alison Wilbur, *Assistant Picture Editor;* Patricia N. Holland, Louisa V. Magzanian, *Senior Researchers;* Deborah J. Cairns, Mary B. Campbell, *Assistant Researchers*

Illustrations and Design: Marianne Rigler Koszorus, Beth Molloy, *Design Assistants;* John D. Garst, Jr., Peter J. Balch, Virginia L. Baza, Charles W. Berry, Lisa Biganzoli, Margaret Deane Gray, Dewey G. Hicks, Jr., Edward J. Holland, Alfred L. Zebarth, *Map Research, Design, and Production*

Far-out Fun: Patricia N. Holland, *Project Editor;* Sue Levin, *Games Artist*

Engraving, Printing, and Product Manufacture: Robert W. Messer, *Manager;* George V. White, *Production Manager;* Raja D. Murshed, June L. Graham, Christine A. Roberts, Richard A. McClure, *Assistant Production Managers;* David V. Showers, *Production Assistant*

Staff Assistants: Debra A. Antonini, Pamela A. Black, Barbara Bricks, Jane H. Buxton, Kay Dascalakis, Mary Elizabeth Davis, Rosamund Garner, Nancy J. Harvey, Jane M. Holloway, Joan Hurst, Suzanne J. Jacobson, Artemis Lampathakis, Cleo Petroff, Katheryn M. Slocum, Suzanne Venino

Interns: Sara A. Grosvenor, Ruth Taswell

Market Research: Joe Fowler, Patrick Fowler, Karen A. Geiger, Cynthia B. Lew, Meg McElligott, Stephen F. Moss

Index: Elizabeth Meyendorff

08736